ROMAN
SOCIAL
RELATIONS

ROMAN
SOCIAL
RELATIONS

50 B.C. TO A.D. 284

RAMSAY MacMULLEN

NEW HAVEN AND LONDON, YALE UNIVERSITY PRESS, 1974

Copyright © 1974 by Yale University.
All rights reserved. This book may not be
reproduced, in whole or in part, in any form
(except by reviewers for the public press),
without written permission from the publishers.
Library of Congress catalog card number: 73–86909
International standard book number: 0-300-01697-2

Designed by Sally Sullivan
and set in Linotype Granjon type.
Printed in the United States of America by
Vail-Ballou Press, Inc., Binghamton, N. Y.

Published in Great Britain, Europe, and Africa by
Yale University Press, Ltd., London.
Distributed in Latin America by Kaiman & Polon,
Inc., New York City; in Australasia and Southeast
Asia by John Wiley & Sons Australasia Pty. Ltd.,
Sydney; in India by UBS Publishers' Distributors Pvt.,
Ltd., Delhi; in Japan by John Weatherhill, Inc., Tokyo.

CONTENTS

PREFACE

My aim in this essay is to get at the feelings that governed the behavior of broad social groups or conditions.

The boundaries around this aim are set by considerations of evidence and focus. The area west of Cirta in Africa, west of Rome's Alpine provinces, yields very little for my purposes; better, therefore, to exclude it altogether. The remaining two-thirds of the empire may not offer a homogeneous unit of study, nor one in all parts equally well illuminated; but it is certainly far better known. As to boundaries of time, I occasionally reach beyond the dates announced in the title, but only for aspects of my subject apparently unaffected by earlier or later developments. For the sake of focus, I exclude relations within the family (in the broad Roman sense of the word): relations of husband with wife, child with parent, master with slave, patron with client. These bear a separate character presenting separate problems. I exclude also race relations, having nothing to add to recent studies.

Many books describe Roman society, and much that
they have to say I must recall where my subject touches,
for example, economic or legal history. From these other
works, however, the present one I hope differs by extend-
ing our knowledge a little farther beyond the upper
classes to the lower, beyond Italy to the provinces, beyond
the city to the countryside, and beyond the external—the
legal and administrative—aspects to the inward. That last
purpose requires direct quotations* so that people may be
heard as often as possible speaking in their own words;
and it explains the mention, on almost every page that
follows, of prejudice, servility, isolation, pride, shame,
friendship, indifference, contempt, loyalty, despair, or
exclusiveness.

That such feelings should be attested now and again,
anyone with imagination could easily guess and even
illustrate from ancient sources. What counts is typicality,
sufficient to shape the conduct of whole strata and thus to
shape events. In a study aiming not at anecdotes and par-
ticularities but at broader statements, it has seemed specially important to make clear whether a given phenomenon was common or not. I have therefore sometimes
multiplied references, not out of pedantry but to show the
basis for my generalizations.

At times it is possible to catch people of the past doing
their own generalizing for us. They may do this in fiction,
when authors try to present a situation that would easily
be believed by their readers, and weave in details felt to be
applicable throughout their own world. Or they may do

* Translations are my own except where otherwise indicated.

this in predictions, as astrologers, dream-diviners, and seers: to stay in business, such practitioners had to deal in probabilities. Or again, we can apply a sort of "association test" to written sources of all kinds, through the study of pairs of words or pairs of ideas: "rich and honored," "rustic and cloddish," "paupers and criminals."

Such, among others, are the devices that must be resorted to in any attempt to understand social feelings and the sense of place in antiquity. But the task is very difficult.

"I can call up spirits from the vasty deep," boasts Shakespeare's Glendower. To which Hotspur replies, "But will they come when you call for them?"

R. MacM.

New Haven
1972

I

RURAL

No one's social relations were so limited and tenuous, so close to no relations at all, as the shepherd's in the hills. His work kept him away from people. In those he did meet he had reason to fear an enemy—which explains a tale told us by a young prince. Out riding one day with his retinue along the lower slopes of the Apennines,

> We had gone a little ways down a road, when, there in the middle, were a lot of sheep in a bunch, at a stand, as happens at narrow places, and four dogs and two shepherds, no one else. Then one shepherd said to the other, "Look you to those riders, they're the ones that do the worst robberies." Hearing this, I spurred my horse and drove into the sheep. They scattered in terror and ambled off hither and yon, baah-ing. The shepherd swung his crook at me, and it landed on the horseman following me. So we took off; and the one that was afraid of losing his sheep lost his crook instead. Do you think this is just a story? It's the truth.[1]

But the truth as Marcus Aurelius saw it, in A.D. 143, sitting astride the best mount money could buy and with enough servants about him to turn the incident into a comedy, was less amusing to the other participants. When they had at last rounded up their flock and put their courage away for the next and perhaps more serious encounter with real brigands, they could exchange a hundred true tales of raids, robberies, and rustling. In its back-country parts, an empire that seemed so civilized, so peaceful, was in fact full of alarms. That accounted for a shepherd's handiness with his staff, and for his dogs—no Border collies but the type of mastiff one may see today in the outskirts of an Anatolian village, regular monsters able to tear a man in pieces.[2]

As to their tough, shaggy, black-tanned masters in hooded cloaks,[3] they lived apart from civilization, leaving hardly a trace of a record on stone. At most they might be remembered in some corner of a hamlet: "Shepherds' Lane."[4] One thought of them in the company of the most miserable outcasts.[5] They were always on the move, for they had to drive their herds from winter to summer pasturage; and in their annual drives or in the uncultivable no-man's land that lay between two villages, they were continually involved in fights about boundaries and rights of transhumance,[6] or lost their animals to thieves. Rustlers, often mounted and armed with swords, gave rise to recurrent complaint matched by recurrent legislation.[7] Presumably they roamed throughout the areas of richest pickings, in the great ranches of Greece for example.[8] But cattle-raising was common and important in Palestine[9]

and other provinces. Italy (to get back to the scene of
Marcus Aurelius' adventure) gives us a document of a
typical kind, except in the fact that it was the emperor
himself who suffered. His agent rehearses the story with
a subordinate:

> The lessees of the flocks under your care in the present case
> are complaining to me of the frequent injury received en
> route through the cattle-drifts, from the police and magis-
> trates of Saepinum and Bovianum, in that animals and
> shepherds, whom they [the lessees] have hired they [the
> police] say are fugitives who have stolen the animals, and
> under this pretext they have driven off the very em-
> peror's sheep.[10]

The year was 170, near the date of another long but fragmentary report posted in Africa. It concerns "complaints
that their fields were destroyed by flocks of sheep . . .
against your will, in order to pasture their herds. . . .
And if a slave has led in herds without his master's
knowledge. . . ." [11] To this latter kind of depredation we
will return below.

Anyone who sketches his mental picture of country life
from Vergil's Eclogues must plainly re-do its outlines to
match real truth. The shepherd was not his own man but
hired to guard someone else's flocks,[12] or a slave: and that
someone else might be removed from him by an immense
distance, physically, as an absentee landlord, socially, by
a wealth that spread its possessions across whole ranges of
hills, and administratively, by the interposition of bailiffs,
overseers, and lessees. Rustic swains had indeed nothing
to sing about. Their world was as poverty-stricken and ig-

nored as it was dangerous. And while Vergil's Lycidas
and Tityrus contested only for priority as poets, their living models had to confront each other, village or city
officials, outraged farmers, or brigands, in struggles that
knew no end.

No one should build his farmhouse near a main road
"because of the depredations of passing travelers." That
was the advice of a man who knew Italy well, at the
height of its peace; while the advice of a contemporary in
Palestine was, if one stopped the night at a wayside inn,
to make one's will.[13] Both warnings came to the same
thing. Away from centers of population, one risked being
robbed or killed. The risk, though varying in degree,
finds mention in written sources of every time and province.[14] Architectural and archeological evidence agrees.
Isolated farmhouses had look-out towers and strong walls
and gates.[15] The less populated countryside throughout
the empire approached a state of endemic warfare, from
which only a stout cudgel, a fast horse, or a well-built
little fortress gave protection.

That was of course not the case where villages or rich
villas dotted a landscape close together. Here, more re-
strained and covert violence prevailed, of the rich against
the poor and of the poor against each other.

Take the rich first. Without trying to decide what percentage of land was in the possession of what percentage
of the population, we would expect to discover big landowners in all areas. Commonly their holdings were scattered. Investors bought whatever happened to come on
the market, wherever they could, as a few rare lists allow

us to see. In second century Attica seventeen persons
owned fifty-eight properties (and five of the seventeen
owned thirty-one).[16] At the same time in Italy, in an area
of perhaps 350 square miles, an inscription names more
than three hundred properties. Among the larger, forty-
seven are given a specific value, of which in turn nineteen
qualified the owner for the rank of municipal councillor
(with 25,000 denarii), five for the equestrian rank (with
100,000 denarii), and four for the senatorial (with 250,000
denarii). Of the forty-seven owners, thirty-seven held
more than one property. One indeed owned twenty-six
properties.[17] A third list farther south gives eighty-nine
properties in the hands of fifty proprietors, seventeen
owning more than one farm, and a single individual
owning as many as eleven.[18] Rich Italians at all periods
put their money into land the length and breadth of the
peninsula,[19] in fact overseas also, to such an extent that the
emperors had to remind them of their allegiance to the
land of their fathers.[20] But similar patterns of scattered
investment governed the provinces. A treatise on sur-
veying tells us that "in many regions we find persons holding lands not contiguous but individual lots in various
places, separated by several holdings." [21]

All of this indicates the extent of absentee ownership, a
phenomenon as well known and attested as any in the
economic history of Rome. A social consequence should
follow. Since obviously the master of several estates could
not visit them all himself and administered them perforce
through bailiffs and accountants, we would expect to find
more irresponsible exploitation on the part of these latter,

vis-à-vis slaves, tenants, hired laborers, and neighbors, than if the master himself had been on the scene. It was easy for him to hurt people he never saw; that he actually did so will appear abundantly in this and the following chapter. In Italy, at least, we can trace a reaction, in the difficulties he encountered in collecting his rents or making a farm pay; sometimes in the heavy loss he suffered.[22]

The landowner tried to consolidate his holdings into a single enormous economic entity for greater efficiency. Cicero, Horace, Seneca, and many other writers censure this ruthless drive toward consolidation so often that one suspects a cliché.[23] It is, however, a phenomenon not peculiar to Italy. The great estates of pasturage in Greece have been noted above, and Pliny the Elder reports that in his day "six landlords owned half of Africa." [24] Empire-wide, the unmistakable effects of this drive are visible in the increasing concentration of rural wealth into fewer hands, a gradual development that needs more study but is unquestioned fact. The details of its procedures can be seen at work in many specific cases. More than buyer and seller on a free market were involved, rather a variety of cruel pressures exerted by the strong against the weak, the arrogant rich, "the powerful," against the adjoining farm, villagers, or "the poor," [25] sometimes by crooked litigation,[26] sometimes by armed force.[27]

A typical instance involves a citizen of Hadrianoutherai on the coast of the province of Asia, toward the mid second century.

There is an estate, the Laneian, not far from the Zeus temple. . . . This estate my kinsmen bought for me while

I was away in Egypt; but certain men of Mysia took it wrongfully, at first uttering every kind of threat and then resorting to actions. Being really desperate . . . , they got together as many servants as they could, and laborers, and came on with weapons of all sorts. Some of them then threw their spears and sling-bullets of clods and stones from a distance while others closed hand-to-hand; some advanced on the house and treated whatever was in it as their own. All was chaos and bloodshed. When report was made of these goings-on, at Pergamum, I was barely in a state to draw breath; but there was a trial. I was at a loss to know what to do.[28]

Still, he managed to represent the matter successfully before the governor's court, and the trial ended with his principal attacker in jail and his own lands secured to him. As in some of the cases Cicero deals with, the offenders here are rich men, using their slaves and tenants as shock troops and picking on a young man, or a sick, or an absent one, as their victim.[29]

Throughout all our evidence, scattered though it is over several centuries, the methods employed and their openness point to the existence of extralegal kinds of power to a degree quite surprising. However majestic the background of Roman law and imperial administration, behold in the foreground a group of men who could launch a miniature war on their neighbor—and expected to get away with it! If we looked beyond our period to the second half of the fourth century, we would see (for example, in Libanius' Forty-Seventh Oration or in certain chapters of the Theodosian Code) only the further development of predatory arrogance long latent in the pax Romana. In earlier centuries it was by no means accepted as a fact of life; but it revealed in a physical way certain broad and common disparities in strength among the various conditions of people.

For the aggressor, impunity depended not so much on the absence of law enforcement as on the presence of force above the law: in a word, influence. How did he get this? How did he exercise it? These questions can be easily followed out among the upper classes, especially through the private letters of Cicero, Pliny, and Fronto, and through a vast body of indirect evidence. The key terms are familiar: patron, client, and "connections" with those private individuals who had some hold over witnesses, plaintiffs, clerks, or with jurymen, governors, municipal magistrates—all friends to the aggressor, all "cousins whom he reckons up by dozens." We need not repeat the investigations of other scholars at this level.[30]

In the lower strata of society, however, Egyptian papyri shed a unique light on aggression. They usually come to us in the form of complaints registered with local authorities, in such a document as this:

To Dioscorus, overseer of the fifth district, from Isodorus son of Ptolemaeus from the village of Karanis. I possess over eighty *arouras,* for which, though they are not sown, I have for long paid the dues to the treasury, and for this reason I have been reduced to poverty. For I experienced great difficulty in sowing, with enormous toil and expense, only eight of these in corn and two in grass-seed. So, when at the time of their growth Ammonas son of

Capeei, Sambathion son of Syrion, Sotas son of Achilles, and Ptollas son of Ariston let their cattle loose on the corn-crops and devoured them, on that occasion also I sent you a petition on the subject. But later, when the crops had grown and put forth their fruit and reached ripeness, before they were harvested, again the same persons, plotting against me and possessing great influence in the neighborhood and wanting me to desert my home, set the same cattle upon the crop and let it be completely devoured, so that nothing at all could be found there. Further, there was Harpalus the shepherd, too: he let his beasts loose on the grass-crop and the hay that had been cut and lay in the field, and they devoured it. And therefore I am unable to keep silence, since the headmen have frequently given instructions that the beasts caught damaging other people's crops should be sold and half of the proceeds should go to the treasury and the other half to the victim of the damage.[31]

We can pick out the details that will recur elsewhere: herds that make trouble, just as in Italy and Greece,[32] and the influential person who hopes to deprive some poor man of his land.

Another set of documents here pieced together into a single file adds further characteristic elements: the vulnerability of property when its owner was away, the invitation to violence that a physical weakness seemed to offer, and the abuse of their authority by local officials:

To the prefect of Egypt from Gemellus of Antinoe, landholder at Karanis. Some time ago, my lord, our father died, leaving me and my sisters as heirs, and we took over his possessions without opposition from anyone. Likewise it came to pass that my uncle died, and I entered into his property without hindrance. But now Julius and Sotas wrongfully, with violence and arrogance, entered my fields after I had sown them and hindered me therein through the power which they exercise in the locality, contemptuous of me on account of my weak vision and wishing to get possession of my property. Then Sotas died and his brother Julius, also acting with the violence characteristic of them, entered the fields that I had sown and carried away a substantial quantity of hay; not only that, but he also cut dried olive shoots and heath plants from my olive grove. When I came there at the time of the harvest I learned that he had committed these transgressions. In addition, not content, he again trespassed with his wife and a certain Zenas, intending to hem in my cultivator with malice so that he should abandon his labor. . . . [And, two years later] I appeal, my lord, against Kastor, tax collector's assistant of the village of Karanis. This person, who held me in contempt because of my infirmity—for I have only one eye and I do not see with it though it appears to have sight, so that I am utterly worthless in both—first publicly abused me and my mother, after maltreating her with numerous blows and demolishing all four doors of mine with an ax so that our house is wide open and accessible to every malefactor—although we owed nothing to the fiscus, and for this reason he dared not even produce a receipt, lest he be convicted through it of injustice and extortion.[33]

Finally, a collection of the most common features among some seventy such pleas for justice, ranging from the first to the fourth century but concentrated in the period from the early first to the later second. To begin with, note the recurrence of physical outrage, the beatings, maulings, and murders.[34] They may accompany a robbery (thefts being frequent) [35] or play a part in intimidation. The plaintiff may allege an attempt to drive him clean out of the village; [36] his enemies want his land, or access to water, which was scarce.[37]

To collect a debt, he may ignore the law to take personal action; so may an enemy, to inflict some further hurt after the verdict has gone against him.[38] The accused often acts in a family group, women not excluded. Self-help is invoked by both the righteous and the criminal.[39] That being the case, we expect to find women especially among the victims—widows, wives whose husbands are away, but also orphans and minors.[40] They call attention to their state as "weak," "without resources," "with no one to turn to" (aboethetos). And of course they (or for that matter, anyone) will be most exposed to attack when they are away from home, on the road. Inhabitants of other villages are likely to prove hostile.[41]

We would like to know what exactly is meant by the recurrent description of someone as "powerful." What of ✓ an accused, "former Exegete of the town of Arsinoe, who possesses a great deal of influence in the villages through his arrogance and violence; and I shall be unable to oppose him before a [local] jury of this kind, for he is very influential." Even the son of a gymnasiarch on appeal to the Strategos failed to obtain justice from this man. He "relies on the prestige of his office, enjoying great power in the villages."[42] And (the plaintiff continues) he is rich, and an extortionate usurer who has already received the principal of the loan and half again as much in interest. A sort of Mafia type emerges, exuberantly formidable, brutal, and threatening. He adds the extra leverage of his wealth, like many other wrongdoers,[43] to his rank among officials, who also figure in our evidence among the oppressors. They apparently conspire to "shake down" the defenseless [44] without excuse or in the name of tax collection.[45]

Brute strength, then, counted for much in the minor quarrels of the village. The only defense lay in one's family. Had government been more easily reached, had officials cared more, no doubt their subjects would not have taken the law into their own hands. Still, some members of a small community constitute natural centers of disturbance. Ptolemaios of Theadelphia, for example, left behind a rich record of his feuds with men of high station; along with his son, he was charged with robbery, and, along with his brother, he died in a fight.[46]

Economic weight counted, too. It is hard to generalize about a whole province over a long span of generations, especially a province presenting such a varied history in so deep a fabric of documentation; for all that, Roman Egypt strikes one as a land of much suffering, in which the only constant element was poverty. True, we know relatively little about Alexandria and the few cities of middling size. Papyri come from and deal with smallish towns and villages. On the other hand, these latter *were* the Nile valley. Dirt poor from cradle to an early grave (their life expectancy being miserably low),[47] fellahin struggled to secure a bare subsistence. Hence the power of those few among them who managed to accumulate some small means, a few fields to lease out, a few jobs to offer at harvest-time, a few rooms or a house to rent, or money to lend at interest.

Although we will never approach an overall estimate of property distribution with any exactness of numbers even in this one area that we know best, there are glimpses of poverty to be caught in scattered statistics. The student who first penetrates the thickets of papyri from Roman Egypt will be struck by the use of the most minute fractions in census returns: a sixty-fourth part of the standard unit of land measurement, the *aroura,* is evidently a possession very well worth recording; the sixth part of a single olive tree; the tenth part of an adobe house. And in that tenth part may be living twenty-six people; in another house, a man, his wife, their six children, two daughters-in-law, three grandchildren, a sister-in-law, her two children, a tenant, his wife and child and in-laws, to a total of twenty-four; in a third dwelling, a man, his brother, two sisters, and five cousins.[48] The custom of exposing unwanted children is well attested in Roman Egypt, small wonder! But we should note a further consequence of the most wretched overcrowding: with everybody living on top of each other, the rate of illegitimacy seems to have hovered around 10 percent.[49] Not that an unwanted child always died. Left on the village dungheap (and thereafter for life registered to that spot as his birthplace) he might be taken up and reared into servitude by a family that had food to spare. Nothing was wasted in the ancient world: not an abandoned baby, not the cloth that kept the ragpicker in business, not the empty fisherman's shack on the beach, not even the grains of barley in horse manure on the streets. There were always people poor enough to fight over another's leavings.[50]

A last statistic: annual unearned income qualifying a man for the high office of Elder. In different villages the sum varied from 200 to 800 drachmai, the number of appointees from four to twelve. Minimum required to stay alive per annum: about 250 drachmai. But even so, there were times and places in which qualified candidates could not be found. However these figures are added, they point to wretched deprivation.[51]

Before moving on to a discussion of the structure of rural communities, however, it might be useful to glance at some quite modern and therefore much better studied villages lying within our chosen geographical area, from Sardinia to Syria. Compressed into a composite form, they may suggest the details that our ancient evidence only allows us to guess at.[52] Analogies, to be sure, prove nothing, but they comfort conjecture.

As an economic unit of a few hundreds up to as many as ten thousand, the central and eastern Mediterranean village has nothing to offer but its land. A small minority of the population can take care of basic trades and crafts, but the more proficient among them drift off to the better markets of the city; a few complex but necessary skills reach the village through traveling artisans, as do certain goods. The adjoining village, however, yields the same crops and has the same needs and surpluses. Most buying and selling is therefore done in the city, in frequent short visits.

Among the peasants there is little differentiation in earning power. The rudimentary tasks of the fields are easily mastered by all. Only the goatherds and shepherds constitute a separate and lower class. Land itself, at the moment when a new community came into being, lay under private ownership, all except common pasturage (or common ponds, streams, and copses). Individual successes and failures, however, tend toward its concentration in the hands of a few. A farmer after a bad year of illness or crop destruction by animals, or after the bursting of his irrigation ditches in a spring flood, borrows at usurious rates, and he and his family are soon obliged to sell out and become tenants or sharecroppers. A bailiff is now their master since, more often than not, the new owner himself lives in the city. A villager who "makes it" aspires to a life of urban idleness, and emigrates; the city man with money to invest buys into one of the villages nearby, comes to own it entire, or owns pieces of property in a number of villages.

Economic ties between urban and rural centers are thus of the closest. They are not friendly. The two worlds regard each other as, on the one side, clumsy, brutish, ignorant, uncivilized; on the other side, as baffling, extortionate, arrogant. Peasants who move to a town feel overwhelmed by its manners and dangers and seek out relatives or previous emigrants from the same village to settle among.

Rent- or tax-collectors who come out to the country face a hostile reception and can expect attempts to cheat and resist them, even by force. They respond with their own brutality. It is just such confrontations with an external enemy—government officials, landlords' agents, crop damage by herds, or a quarrel over land or water with people of another locality—that unite the village.

Internally, the village is by no means united. While the majority of its inhabitants trace their descent to a handful of original lines, are thus attached in a vague way to numerous kin, and choose a wife within the community, the nuclear families are forever bickering with each other, fighting, and competing for advantage. Their houses' blank walls and the twisting streets allow some privacy; but everyone keeps as close an eye as he can on his neighbors. Gossip is perpetual, and the market in the center or the unavoidable use of common water fountains, baking ovens, threshing floors, or oil presses encourages a kind of jealous nosiness.

Poorer families may crowd together in a single dwelling, embracing married sons and daughters and occasionally cousins in large units. A typical household will however consist of no more than a half-dozen people under a clearly marked head, the father. They work in the fields together. To this unit as to traditional village customs everyone owes the strongest loyalty. Deviation and individualism find little scope. Heads of households in a very small community constitute a ruling body of elders. In larger ones, it is a combination of strong personality and strong clan support that produces a leader.

He prefers to keep communal affairs in his own control, not to refer them to city authorities.

Our "model village," as it emerges from the shared features of a score of modern examples, shares features also with the Egyptian. Some of the analogies with what has already been described are too obvious to need any signpost. Others will suggest themselves as we return to the sketch of our proper subject, the Roman period.

At the very outset of their rule over Egypt, the emperors raised village officials to a position directly responsible for their local taxes and corvées, displacing the Ptolemaic bureaucracy at that level, and eventually made these same officials answerable for the entire territory within their boundaries, thus displacing the Ptolemaic categories of centrally administered nonprivate land.[53] Successive changes thus encouraged the development of community, principally in an economic sense. It was as a Farmers' Collective that the village found tenants to work vacant fields, labor to clear the irrigation system, guards to watch the crops, or shepherds to lease the common pasturage.[54] Herders, like other groups engaged in one and the same business, for their part spontaneously formed themselves into associations headed by Elders or by similar officers bearing other titles; so also the Fishermen or the Carpenters of the village So-and-So under their Elders, the Tenants of imperial estates with their Secretary, the Weavers under their President.[55] As we might expect, only the occupations involving the most people gave rise to associations—and, incidentally, to personal names, just as today we know persons called Carpenter, Taylor, Coward (Cow-herd), or Weaver.[56] Sections of villages told where they lived: Goosefarmers' Quarter, or Shepherds', or Linen-Weavers'.[57] In the smallest rural centers, a single urge is discovered at many levels, drawing together the whole or its most prominent and ubiquitous crafts or pursuits into social union.

The institutional shape assumed by strong shared interests at first sight seems to invite an economic interpretation. Peasants are corporately responsible for the delivery of certain goods and services to the provincial government, and leave the clearest surviving trace of their existence in receipted deliveries of taxes or approved nominations to some burdensome duty. Over the course of centuries, in fact, pressure from the state slowly compacted peasants into tighter and tighter corporations for a purely economic reason, to wring from them an increasing tribute. Similarly, subgroups like shepherds or sharecroppers show themselves to us through agreements to extract a yield from village resources or to pay license fees for the exercise of a craft. Appearances, however, are misleading. The associative principle looks like an economic one simply because a barely literate society naturally put on paper only things like contracts and receipts. Exact obligations had to be set down in writing. But the dominance of business matters among papyri distorts the total record. Actually, unions were not formed for an economic end, they were merely handy to that purpose once formed. It is almost unheard of for the Shepherds' Association or any other to control admission to their ranks or their rate of pay, or to deal with some similar problem by joint action.[58] Any analogy with a medieval guild or modern labor union is wholly mistaken.

Rather, their purpose is social in the broadest sense. The same few hundreds or thousands that the state looked on as a single whole to yield it taxes, looked on themselves as the Village Society that celebrated the two-day festival of Isis or the ten-day festival of Bacchus. Their president, who hired entertainers and ordered the supplies, sometimes bore a title that further expressed his duties. He was the *klinarch,* "in charge of tables." Even in Rome, Juvenal knew of

> the happy, merry day, at festal times, and the joy of great banquets, the tables spread in temple precincts and street crossings, the couches set out for the whole night, and the sun of seven days rising and setting on them. Egypt is no doubt a repellent country but, as I myself have noted, the self-indulgence of its barbarous throngs [in the villages] equals that of the notorious [city of] Canopus.[59]

The party mood spread downward from the community to its parts. Associations of some single craft were guests of a rich benefactor or tapped their members for dues to buy beer and food and to secure from the nearest town the services, for a week, of traveling troupes of castanet dancers, trumpeters, flute-players, tumblers, or clowns. Torches lit up the nocturnal scene, daylight saw it still in motion. Presents were exchanged, altars and friends wreathed in roses, the diners beautifully drunk and dizzy with the noise and dancing. Nor did Isis or Bacchus yield to the regular routine of the harvest. That was suspended, on a landowner's fields, while the organizations of his laborers celebrated the day. He bought their wine, he paid the piper. But the flutist hired to play at vintage worked for *him,* since music speeded the treading of the grapes.[60]

Against the evidence of jealousy, violence, feuds, and conspiracies that divided an Egyptian village (above, pp. 8–12), and the clustering of various parts of its population into clubs and corporations for social purposes, we must set the contrary evidence of the community as a whole joining in gigantic parties. When tension relaxed, when there was something to think about beyond the often desperate scramble for too little space, too little food, or too little water, nearness gave rise to fraternity. Their very deficiencies contributed to the same effect. They were likely to set apart only one threshing floor that they all used, and to build only one great storage barn for their grain taxes.[61] Individual resources would not stretch to these facilities. And they needed each other for company and the exchange of small goods and small items of news. That brought them into the streets. There they would find the scribe to supply their lack of schooling, ready to write contracts, letters, and receipts for his illiterate neighbors.[62] Those who sought his help in the afternoon doubtless learned all they wanted to know about the affairs of his morning customers.

At the same time, the community was penetrated by outsiders. Real wealth in Egypt was centered in the vast city of Alexandria, from which it reached out in the form of investments and leases to the back-country—to little Theadelphia (population about 2,500), for example,

where in the first century more than two-thirds of the
vineyard and garden land belonged to ten Roman citizens
and eighty-seven Alexandrians. A further substantial part
of village lands would be held, and some temporarily
rented, by citizens of the district capitals.[63] These owners
occasionally visited the local scene to find new tenants or
check up on their holdings, but generally their bailiffs
did all this for them. Absentee landlordism had its tides
and changes, which it is not our job to describe; but
throughout our period it is always true to say that the
bulk of real property belonged not to the peasant but to
someone who did no work himself and who, more often
than not, lived elsewhere. When he did appear, it was as
a master; when he took up residence, local office was his
natural due.[64]

Another representative village, Philadelphia, is well
enough known to provide statistics about outsiders of a
different sort. With a population of a few thousands and
a taxpayer roll of about twelve hundred, 10 percent of the
latter were in the first century drawn from other points of
residence: some, small artisans, shepherds, donkey-drivers,
and peddlers; others, laborers and lessees.[65] In exchange,
5 percent of Philadelphia's folk were off on business of
one kind or another in Alexandria, not permanently, and
an additional 20 percent at other villages or district capitals.[66]

Peasants tended to remain peasants down the generations,[67] but in bad times a proportion varying according
to the degree of famine, inadequate Nile flooding, or tax
pressure wandered off into vagabondage and laborer

status,[68] and there was of course some village industry, above all, weaving. Migrant or harvest labor we will come to later (below, pp. 42 f.).

While it is hard to generalize about mobility in rural √ Egypt, it is at least clear that those who would deny it altogether are wrong. It is an out-of-date, city-dwellers' view that sees the life of farming hamlets as absolutely static. On the other hand, we should distinguish between what biologists would call Brownian movement, carrying the small farmer from place to place on short trips, short contracts, and short business errands, without changing his fundamental condition, and opposed to this the more significant movement of perhaps a tenth of the rural population. That would include people mobile both socially and physically: petty traders, the owners of petty workshops in basic industries, craftsmen, entertainers, and the begging poor (for mobility may be downward as well as upward). What prevented mobility from offering much hope was the concentration of rural wealth in the hands of absentee landlords, who drew off from the land whatever surplus it afforded. Some went to taxes, some to the urban market. A peasant boy had small chance at it, however he changed the work he did or the place where he lived.

I have now described very sketchily the kind of life and relations to be found in nineteenth- and twentieth-century villages of the Mediterranean—the most easily studied— and the data from papyri, which for the ancient world are relatively abundant but far less satisfactory, of course, than data of more modern periods. Finally, we turn to the most scattered sources of all, those that tell us a little about villages in the Near East.

Their formal structure, considered from the outside, recalls that of Greek cities, their envied and prestigious models. Inscriptions of the eastern Roman provinces reveal a sort of chief magistrate or magistrates, a council, and a body of inhabitants expressing their will in assembly.[69] Candidates for office, just as in cities, might be required to contribute a minimum sum to the year's expenses of the community, the few examples of this practice representing what would be in local terms a sizable sum: 250 denarii in 213-4, 1000 denarii sixty years later, as √ a result of galloping inflation;[70] but a more common variant was the understanding, likewise typical of cities, that whoever was voted into office should show his sense of the honor by paying for some needed facility or resource.[71] In effect, he bought the title of Arbiter, First Villager, Overseer, Local Leader, or however he might by styled.[72] In territories owned by the crown he might be the imperial slave or freedman set up as bailiff. Otherwise he was one of the absentee landowners often distinguished as a special category.[73]

The Council of Elders, sometimes called Senators in imitation of their grander urban models, in some villages dispensed with magistrates and ran things themselves.[74] A representative text from second-century Lydia shows them in action:

> In the village of Kastollos of [the city] Philadelphia, at a public meeting presided over by the Board of Elders and with all the other villagers, they considered how to divide

up their land in individual lots, in the location called
Agathon's Sheepfolds, where it is hilly, as to which the
villagers . . .[75]

which we may compare with a still more fragmentary inscription from southern Syria:

Resolved by the people of Korinos village, with their common consent, that no villager . . . in the common land,
that is on Mount Danaba, neither a threshing floor nor
anything (planted?) . . . according to our usage; and if
anyone . . .[76]

Both resolutions present the inhabitants in the act of
reaching joint decisions about important business. They
speak with one voice, just as we find them elsewhere calling themselves simply and collectively "the farmers," "the
people," "the commune of such-and-such a village."[77]
They jointly own and legally inherit property,[78] and together meet for periodic fairs. In the fourth century a
resident of Antioch looked out from his city to the surrounding

large villages, populous no less than many cities, and with
crafts such as are in towns, exchanging with each other
their goods through festivals, each playing host in turn
and being invited and stimulated and delighted and enriched by them through giving of its surplus or filling its
needs, setting out some things for sale, buying others, in
circumstances far happier than seaboard markets. In the
place of the latters' waves and swells, they transact their
business to laughter and handclapping.[79]

The happy sound is echoed from the northwest areas of
Asia and Bithynia. Inscriptions speak of village wine

parties there to which the inhabitants or their rich patron contributed food and drink and wreaths, hiring a little orchestra and providing lamps and candles to carry the rejoicing through the night.[80] If the costs proved too heavy or the occasion honored a deity of wide cult, several villages would combine.[81] Religious festivals brought the greatest crowds together, of which traders naturally took advantage. And traders, along with traveling craftsmen, kept even isolated hamlets in touch with each other.[82]

In the western half of our area of study, villages are most easily studied in Africa Proconsularis and in central Italy. The smaller ones had closely crowded houses in Italy just as they did in Egypt; in Africa, they had big central storage barns as they did in Syria or Egypt.[83] Italian peasants, like their equivalents in other provinces, passed on their immemorial drudgery to their children,[84] finding the ties of their indebtedness no less strong than those of habit and attachment to their ancestral acres. Communally regulated lands and water for irrigation are known in Africa.[85] Both there and in Italy, community government leaves its traces on stone, in inscriptions that mention magistracies, Councils, and meetings of various forms. Details need not concern us—only the impulse found universally in the empire to rise to the shape of a fully accredited city.[86] Connections with the richer outside world were kept up by villages through the same means that cities themselves used: influential patrons. Those of villages were of course sometimes the highest authority of all, the emperors, in vast crown estates; but otherwise, decurions of a neighboring municipality, retired army officers, or the like, who could be counted on to pay for some public building or social occasion.[87] The prominence of persons specified as "estate-owners," their separation as a class by themselves, and sometimes their identification with the village ruling body, all hint at the equivalence of wealth and influence binding villages to the nearest urban aristocracy.[88] We will return to this subject in the next chapter. On the whole, however, on patronage as on the other matters just reviewed, we are less well informed than in the Greek-speaking areas. At best, isolated glimpses blend into the much clearer landscape of Syria or Egypt, and they in turn into the living scene that meets the traveler there today.

Readers will sense everywhere in the foregoing one obvious deficiency: the peasant too seldom speaks for himself. We would like to hear him say, "Here is where I fit in, these are my feelings toward my neighbors or toward outsiders, such-and-such are the groups in which I feel at home, or depend on, or compete against; my prospects, my condition, my social heritage, are thus-and-so." Instead, either he has left us only brief mentions of the externals of his life, or appears through the eyes of observers quite alien to him: the literate, or rather the literary, classes. They are not likely to have understood the peasant. Though he supported their own ease and cultivation, he was as silent, motionless, and far below them as the great tortoise on which, in Indian mythology, the whole world ultimately rests.

The hard shell around the peasant community—the fierce dogs, scrutiny of strangers, crop- and field-guards, the sudden stoning of a dangerous outsider by lowering crowds [89]—in fact covered only a pitiful organism. It had, as we will see in the next chapter, no real power to protect itself at all, save against another village or a passing traveler. Any force, economic or administrative, easily penetrated its defenses, abused it, and drained off its resources. Within cowered poverty; as a result, tensions; as relief from both, superstition mixed with wine, beer, dancing, a total forgetfulness in days and nights of festivals honoring Isis, Cybele, Men, Bacchus, or some other deity.

The basic cells of the organism can have been nothing other than families—so much by conjecture, since even for Egypt we lack a study of that institution [90] and none can be attempted for other provinces. Except where poverty required several generations, cousins, and in-laws to live together, it is a nuclear group of a half-dozen that we find most often. Councils of Elders hint at a community run by heads of clans, but for this there is no direct evidence, and the ubiquity of other groups, arranged according to shared occupations, tells against it. The term *Elders* does suggest, however, what is amply attested in many indirect ways, a respect for patrilineal customs, authority, and position in life. That returns us to the central characteristic of villages—their conservatism. They and their population hovered so barely above subsistence level that no one dared risk a change. Conservatism in its root sense, simply to hang on to what one had, was imposed by force of circumstances. People were too poor, they feared to pay too heavy a price, for experiment of any kind. So the tortoise never moved, it never changed its ways.

II

RURAL-URBAN

Ancient writers represented an urban culture, even those few like Plutarch who chose to live most of their lives in a rural setting. From their villas they sent to the city to order books and invite their friends for a visit; to the city they went for their education and submitted their works for applause. Much more typically, writers lived actually in some metropolis: Athens, Rome, Antioch, Smyrna, Alexandria. If they sometimes dealt with the country, they did so either *as* writers, following literary traditions, or as an urban elite, not as citizens (in point of familiar knowledge or attachment) of the scenes they described. The two points of view, traditional and urban, produced utterly conflicting pictures in our sources.

Tradition reaching back to Hesiod and Theocritus offered a favorable view of the country, reinforced by the Romans' particular nostalgia for the days of their ancestors: Cincinnatus and around him a cluster of sturdy yeomen ready at their country's call to drop the plow and seize the sword; just as ready to return after victory to their few acres, tiny cottage, and submissive, pure, laborious wives and children. Seneca falls into raptures over the cramped living quarters contrasted with the boundless moral horizons of the elder Scipio; Apuleius looks with pretended longing on "the little plot of land" and wide virtues of Atilius Regulus, and goes on to say that "a wife is married under far better auspices for her off-spring on a farm than in a town, on a fertile soil than in a sterile place, among the earthy furrows than among the flagstones of the forum. . . . To those ancient Romans Quinctius and Serranus and many others like them, not only wives but consulates and dictatorships were offered among the fields." Cato, in a much read passage, and Cicero, to say nothing of Varro, Vergil and Horace, Columella and Calpurnius Siculus and Juvenal, expand on similar themes.[1]

So did Greek authors of the Empire. Musonius, Dio Chrysostom, Themistius, Libanius, Synesius, sometimes in whole orations (smelling very strongly of the lamp), run through a catalogue of arguments. They dwell most on the moral ones: rustic life accords best with nature, suffices better to itself, lies closer to the ultimate source of all bounty, constitutes the very foundation of ease, plenty, harmony (and cities!). Its delightful scenes soothe and uplift us, its healthy foods protect us to a green old age, its labors leave no leisure for crime or strife. The farmer is "honest and simple," devoted to the cult of the gods that springs so naturally from the rhythms and offerings of the harvest year. He alone knows justice and piety entire —whereas "city evils are a hindrance to philosophizing." "Urban dwellers and anyone else not connected with farming set a positive value on litigation and injustice," on the uproar and quarrelsome atmosphere of the market-place or the imperial court with its intrigues.[2] Hardly a word, incidentally, about the economic contribution that farmers made to the state, not a word about hard work or bad seasons. Against the rhapsodies of these ancient Goldsmiths, the reader must be his own George Crabbe.

And what these same writers have to say in other con-texts, when they have laid aside Hesiod and Theocritus and speak unselfconsciously, much better represents the feelings of their urban world. To Juvenal, for instance, nothing is more ridiculous than the farmer who tries to pass as a product of the schools of urban elegance and cultivation; nothing more different from Dio Chrysos-tom's sense of the fitting, the graceful, the citified, than the clumsy, ill-shorn peasants. Their life, says Cicero, "clashes with the more polished elegance of a man"; and when he wants to vilify his enemies, he terms them "rustics and country folk." So, for that matter, does Apu-leius: "You are, through rustication, an unknown." [3]

Since surviving sources are of course mostly the work of men who valued literature, it is not surprising to find in them many contemptuous references to yokel accents and lack of education.[4] Country folk had read no books, their choice of words was out of date and uncouth, they dropped their aitches; in contrast, *urbanitas,* meaning city fashions but above all those of the capital itself.

That value blended with loyalty to one's whole culture.

A pure Latin was the pride of the ruling race, above the provincial variations that one detected in a man from northern Italy, worse still, from Spain or Africa. One blushed to be detected in an un-Roman slip.[5] Foreign words to be sure crept in; they even gained naturalized status in the course of time; but the emperor Claudius only exaggerated a very common prejudice when he withdrew the grant of citizenship from a man who could not speak good Latin.[6] *Urbanitas* opposed not only *rusticitas* but *peregrinitas* as well.

Similarly the Greeks. Their language had indeed deteriorated terribly, so purists felt, and worst of all in the mouths of those races that Alexander had conquered.[7] We can easily see what distressed the highly educated: the gulf that opened gradually between the prose and poetry of the classical period and what was being written or spoken even in good circles of Roman Athens or Alexandria. But, as inscriptions prove, away from the city each mile marked a further deviation from correctness.[8] When one looks at the documents of an Egyptian village, corruptions are clearer still.[9] In sum, "there is a difference between rustics, semi-rustics, and the inhabitants of cities," as Strabo says; and three centuries later, "how great a distance between city-dwellers and the rural," exclaims St. Gregory of Nazianzus.[10]

Finally, a curious etymological fact, that from one single Semitic root derive (in Syriac, Arabic, Aramaic, and Hebrew) the words for boor, idiot, crude ignorant fellow. The root means literally "outsider," but in fact "outside the city."[11]

To this universal feeling of aloofness and superiority

that city-dwellers expressed we will return later. But it was more than a matter of culture, polish, and choice diction. The peasant was felt to be an unmannerly, ignorant being, in bondage to sordid and wretched labor, and so uncivilized that he could not be called on for the full duties of a citizen.[12] Gone are the scenes of innocence, the purer race, the playful simplicity and healthy life that poets and philosophers found in the fields—all dissolved in the arrogance of a higher civilization.

Occasionally we catch a glimpse of that civilization through the eyes of the country-dweller. It appalled him with its skyscrapers, "the tumult in the city, the shoving, the theater crowds," "a great throng gathered in it, and a marvelous clamor and shouting, so they all seemed to me to be at war with each other."[13] These folk were the peasant's natural enemies, "those who reside in large towns, who indulge in robbery, in adultery, and in vain and false oaths."[14] Yet his own world repelled him, too. If he grew rich, by luck, he saw nothing in farming to be ashamed of. A few epitaphs declare the deceased to have been a good farmer or advertise the tools of his success: a plow in relief or a crude vignette of his property.[15] More often, however (though the evidence is still very sparse), he agreed with his detractors that his was an existence of endless toil.[16]

The difficulties under which the peasant labored are well known, though the modern student from his own experience is not likely to understand them very easily. Between Sardinia and Syria, good farmland is the exception rather than the rule. Fields throw up stones more readily than harvests, soil is shallow, and many areas get too little rain to be of much use. Because of the expense of land transport in antiquity, surpluses could not reach places hit by a bad season. As a result, local shortages and occasional widespread famines turn up in a variety of sources.[17] At Aspendus in the first century a traveler

> found nothing but vetch on sale on the market, and the citizens were feeding on this and on anything else they could get; for the rich had shut up all the grain and were holding it for export from the country; [18]

and a physician in the second century noted more generally how

> among many of the peoples subject to the Romans . . . , those who lived in cities, according to their habit of storing up in the summer sufficient food to last through the whole year, took all the wheat from the fields, along with the barley, beans, and lentils, and left the peasants the leguminous crops which they call "pulses," though they also took a good deal of these too to the city. The country folk, finishing what was left over the winter, had to make do with an unwholesome diet throughout the summer, eating shoots and suckers of trees and bushes, and bulbs and roots of unwholesome plants.[19]

These crises, however, on reflection seem less striking than certain features of everyday life: that sparrows appeared for sale as an item of diet (how many would make a meal?), that the neglected corners of one's fields should by Jewish law be reserved for the poor to glean, and that the man whose daylong and only occupation was to draw up water from wells should be quite taken for granted.[20] A man of that sort lived and died unrecorded, himself and any family he might have being able to afford at most his bare name on a headstone. The nobles whose literary works we read took no notice of his misery.

But peasants were visited by an affliction worse than locusts, worse than drought: the man from the city, come to collect rents or taxes.

"Before the grain-tax is delivered, the poll-tax falls due."[21] "The cities are set up by the state in order . . . to extort and oppress."[22] So say our sources for Palestine, and truly. The central government did indeed delegate to the cities everywhere the gathering in of tribute within their individual territories, and they did indeed shift its weight to the shoulders of the peasants (for ancient writers, though they say far less about this vital subject than we would expect, do take it for granted that taxation will fall most heavily on the farmers).[23] Farmers could only defend themselves by a kind of economic suicide: If your demands drive us to desperation, they said to the officials, then we will flee our fields and you will get no yield at all.[24] It was no empty threat. The only province offering some depth of documentation through its papyri, Egypt, amply confirms a pertinent and significant remark of Varro's, toward the beginning of our period. Speaking of the available supply of landless laborers, he tells us that "those whom we call 'debtors' (*obaerarii*) are to be found in numbers in Asia, Egypt, and Illyricum."[25] We will defer till later the discussion of these laborers and pass over the many studies of *anachoresis,* meaning flight from one's fields, village, debts, and creditors, in Egypt. There is furthermore the long, well-attested history of the government's struggles to encourage the farming of abandoned land, too well known (especially through texts of Hadrian's reign) to need a survey here. It obviously indicates in various times and regions a level of profitability in agriculture close to zero. Add to it another phenomenon, the remission of back-dues accompanied by the burning of government records, not so much from the rulers' beneficence as from the sheer inability of their subjects, over repeated years of failure, to keep up their payments. Making the best of a bad job, the government wiped its books clean, advertised the ceremony as an act of pure bounty through pictures on the coinage, bas-reliefs on public buildings, or proclamations posted in the marketplace—and began again from scratch.

Most conclusive testimony of all, however, are the tax revolts or outbreaks mostly of that character that required the action of provincial garrison armies—revolts for which the evidence has never been carefully gathered and studied but which reveal in rough outline a common pattern of desperation: first, initial conquest by the Romans; next, the rapid confiscation of all hidden weapons; then, the assessment by the conquerors of what they have gained so as to exploit its riches methodically; the consternation of the censused; and thereafter recurrent spasms of protest against the weight of tribute harshly calculated and still more harshly exacted.[26] Though the provincial cities were spared and along with the whole of Italy enjoyed many flourishing centuries, though they constitute the triumph of Roman civilization and receive the chief emphasis in any book about the empire, still, the stirrings beneath them serve as a reminder of a different, less happy rural world.

The several kinds of evidence just reviewed combine to prove that the Romans wrung ultimately from the provincial peasants all that could be economically extracted. This was not done without pain and protest. Despairing of mercy from intermediate agents, cries rose direct to the emperor from quite tiny places: an islet in the Aegean (Astypalaea), the fishermen of Gyaros who found themselves unable to scrape together 150 denarii per year, or the tenant farmers of some single crown estate.[27] When their pleas were heard, that was news. Rejection naturally never was recorded. If it is an argument from silence, however, to conclude from these appeals that taxes bore down very heavily, we can turn to scattered complaints of another kind. "We are beaten with sticks and cudgels," say the plaintiffs; we suffer "many tortures" and "blows of the fist"; "the rack and the scourge crack." An observer of the 30s in Judaea recalls the sufferings inflicted

a little time ago in our own district by a person who was appointed to serve as collector of taxes. When certain debtors from poverty took flight in fear of some terrible retribution, he led off by force their women, children, parents, and other kin, and beat them and abused them and inflicted every kind of outrage on them to reveal where the fugitive had gone or to pay what he owed—though they could do neither, the one from ignorance, the other from greater poverty than the fugitive's. He did not give

up until he had wrung their bodies with the rack and
scourge and ended their lives with unheard of afflictions.
. . . When there were no kin left, the outrage was extended to their neighbors and at times to whole villages
and towns, which were quickly abandoned and emptied
of inhabitants.[28]

It is quite by chance that this particular report reaches us
from the early Empire. Later, evidence becomes a little
fuller. No wonder, then, that the villager lied about his
savings for the year, took his beatings as best he could,
and "would blush if he did not, in consequence of re-
fusing tribute, show many stripes on his body."[29] A
regular war, this, carried on between the rural inhabitants
who had nothing but their powers to endure, and the tax
collector backed by the ultimate powers of the state.

From the victim's point of view taxes and rents came to
the same thing. Sometimes it is hard to make out just
which is meant in a petition or outcry. The high percentage of land owned by absentee landlords and their
residence in cities have been recalled in earlier pages (pp.
5 f., 20 f.); it was their agents or themselves that appeared
for a share of the crop at harvest time. The same land-
holders also enjoyed the necessary minimum wealth and
standing in the eyes of their fellow citizens to be elected
municipal magistrates, thereby assuming responsibility
for whatever the city and its territory owed to Rome.
Thus they appeared in a doubly oppressive role.

As landlords, their practice of hoarding crops to sell in
a time of shortage and high prices emerges in the two
passages already quoted (page 33), one belonging to

the first and the other to the second century. Both have the tone of generalization; but it is nothing more than a guess how common such murderous greed as they show may have been. Certainly Pliny the Younger and other landowners of his circle represented a very different morality, in Italy of the early second century, and not only there but in the provinces as well, archeology turns up chance traces of a sort of rural middle class, living in small but reasonably comfortable houses and with fair-sized holdings to support them.[30] The third and fourth centuries, however, brought a change. The hoarding of grain for a rise in price and usurious loans to those who lacked food and seed corn seem to have grown more common.[31] This fits with another, equally gradual and much better attested change from independent clusters of rural inhabitants to what may be called monopolized villages.

The general background is easy to describe. Beginning at about the birth of Cicero, the tendency of the empire's socioeconomic development over five centuries can be compressed into three words: fewer have more. That story would make a good book—and a big one. It would take account of the grand villas found around Lake Balaton in Pannonia, behind Carthage in Africa, near Antioch in Syria, wherever one looks. Each one required the yield of a wide, wide area of intensive agriculture. The chance of marriage connections or investment might concentrate into a single pair of hands control over not scores of families but hundreds, not hundreds of acres but thousands. We have then a village or villages monopolized.

A process with many variations: It might begin with

the opening up of marginal or abandoned land by a city man with money to sink into the project. His efforts would attract tenants and laborers, raising a jumble of cottages destined to grow into a hamlet of some size.[32] Alternatively, a region of declining fortunes where land was easy to buy might be absorbed by members of some rich clan and their ultimate inheritor find himself master of all.[33] However it happened, the process tended toward the virtual or entire ownership of a village by a single estate.

Evidence for the end product, when collected,[34] dots the map of every part of the empire. The phenomenon could hardly be more widespread. And the master treated these villages as he was entitled to in law, as if the living community, its individual members, and its energies were his to do with as he wanted: to sell the whole, donate its rents to some public purpose, set up at its center a periodic market that dominated its little economy, or assign its inhabitants to any job he had in mind.[35]

Landlords likewise administered justice over their peasants. After all, governors on assize came round irregularly. Their courts involved unpredictable delays and responded to unpredictable influences. Also, they cost a lot, if an advocate had to be hired. As a far more convenient alternative, then, litigants in the Lydian back-country might be found joined in a sort of medieval challenge and counter-challenge, taking oaths in the jealous presence of a local deity.[36] The Jews had their Sanhedrin, of course, but they also had autonomous courts scattered through Judaea and Galilee, properly with three men on the bench but sometimes usurped by a single big property-owner as judge, and with a reputation for oppressive and venal verdicts.[37] Greek law allowed for the settlement of disputes, typically family ones concerning such matters as bequests and property, by private arbitration, and we see the procedure in operation in Egypt and Greece of the Empire.[38] Roman law, at least as we see it in Italy, had similar provisions. Boundary disputes continually caused bad blood, and "an umpire, agreed on" (as the form goes, *arbiter ex compromisso*) would be chosen to adjudicate.[39] But other kinds of cases could be heard in the same way, apparently quite often, since the relevant section of the Digest is a bulky one and one text speaks of "frequent" recourse to the system.[40] Our interest focuses on the kind of men picked as arbiters. They were to be "good men"; but we will see later (pp. 116 f.) just what that meant in the minds of the ruling classes. Less ambiguously, they were big landowners with high social connections: Pliny and Plutarch (the former especially in the country districts where he had his holdings), the *patroni* of a town (Pompeii), the richest lessee of local lands (in Pisidian Pogla), or an ex-praetor retired to the little town of Histonium on the Adriatic.[41] Long before the famous chapter of the Theodosian Code (11.24, A.D. 360–415), "On Patronage Exercised over Villages," big landowners are seen adding jurisdiction to their other powers of control.

To touch skippingly on this complicated and obscure aspect of legal history and to bring forward only a half-dozen illustrations from a perfectly miscellaneous set of sites, some with a background of Greek institutions, some

with a quite different Roman background, meets no-
body's criteria of exact scholarship. I may as well insert
here, as I might at almost every point in this essay, my
sense of frustration in describing matters taken for
granted among the contemporaries of the Empire and
therefore little reported—matters which (as the ancients
would have said) were undignified, contributed nothing
to their sense of what counted, and therefore were seldom
mentioned in their proper works of literature. We catch
only random hints. At best they are suggestive.

One thing they suggest, however, is reassuring. Under-
neath the surface variations in terminology, most institutions we deal with betray strong family resemblances no
matter in what province they are studied. Though time
and place make a difference, the many words in Greek
and Latin that designate a hamlet dissolve into a single
legitimate object of study, since the hamlet itself arose as
an answer to universal needs. Similarly, the terms vary
for village headman, a figure to organize and speak for
the community conveniently but who required the support of an oligarchy—of Elders, or however *they* might
be named. Organization of some sort was inevitable. That
it should avail nothing against armies, first, and then
against the forces latent in cities, whether military, political, or economic, is a fact ubiquitous in the empire. And
the forces attaining their height in urban centers naturally
drew off from the countryside as much as possible of all
that men valued: influence and command over tenants of
a villa, over a hamlet, over a village swollen to some
thousands of inhabitants; wealth, in the form of agri-

cultural products and services; amenities and skills, by which the level of urban civilization was raised to another plane altogether. The inhabitants of that higher civilization looked down on the peasant. From Rome, Alexandria, Carthage, or Antioch, they scorned his almost barbarous manners. The easier in conscience, then, to mistreat him. Hence the ruthless measures of rent- and tax-collection by "men of the arm," in the expressive slang of Judaea,[42] which drained the land, kept it poor, and increased the chances of a city-dweller's finding a bit for sale. In chapter I, the concentration of holdings by rough methods was sketched; in the present chapter, the passing of entire villages into one man's hands.

Even in Italy the margins of profit in agriculture were ordinarily not very generous. Estates being run as businesses could not afford a crowd of idle hands, so landlords kept their work force to the minimum, at need recruiting free labor. Special skills (smiths, carpenters, physicians, fullers, wagoners for transport, etc.) reached them from cities, as we might expect;[43] surprisingly, much unskilled labor did as well.[44] Vintage needed the most outside help; ditch-digging, cutting hay, and harvesting wheat or olives were contracted for also.[45] In Italy, major seasonal migrations brought laborers into the richer agricultural areas at harvest time.[46] Their position as regards their employer would often be protected by contract, if they hired out in gangs,[47] but singly they were absorbed into the estate's work team unprotected, quite on a level with slaves.[48]

From such migrant groups, one success story reaches us

in the form of a verse-epitaph set up in the fair-sized country town of Mactar in Africa. In the deceased's day, the third century, the country thereabouts specially flourished. He rode a tide of prosperity to its height, over a life-span of seventy years or more, though he was, as he says,

> born of a poor, small family—my father lacked income-property or house. From the day of my birth I have spent my life working in my fields—never a rest for them or myself. When the year brought forth the ripened grain, then was I the first to cut the stalks. When the team of harvesters had gone out to the fields with their scythes, whether seeking fields to mow in Numidian Cirta or of Jove, I as harvester was ahead of all others, the first in the fields, leaving their close ranks behind me. I reaped twelve harvests under the raging sun and then, from laborer, became contractor, and for eleven years commanded the teams of harvesters. Our hand cut the Numidian fields. This work, and a life content with little, availed to make me master of a home with a farmstead—a home that lacks no riches. Our life won the fruits of office, too: I, even I, was enrolled among the city senators, and chosen by them to sit in the house of that body. From a small farm boy I, even I, became censor. I fathered and lived to see sons and dear grandsons. I have passed through years distinguished by the merits of my career—years that an evil tongue never hurt with any accusation. Learn, mortals, how to live without accusations. Thus have I deserved to die as I lived, honestly.[49]

Heavy labor did it, under the broiling sun—that and good character. He reminds us of the elder Cato; better, of the person honored in a more fragmentary inscription from another country town, in northern Italy. From pride in his occupation, he took or accepted the nickname Farmer:

a patron of good freedmen—most of all, of those who work well and hard in the fields and take good care of their bodily vigor, which is essential for farmers; who eat nourishing food and preserve every other resource they may have. Take all this as true advice, whoever wants to live really well and freely: first, to show respect where it is due; next, to desire your master's good; honor your parents; earn others' trust; neither speak nor listen to slander. Whoever harms or betrays no one will lead a pleasant life, uprightly and happily, giving no offense. These are the sayings that Farmer taught us to remember, himself taught by his own nature and practice, not by learned men.[50]

The tone of these injunctions is very much that of a master who expected his full due from slaves and freedmen: hard work, of course, is the note most struck, but beyond that, deference also. A third text suggests what that might mean, though the peasants who are speaking refer to some problem that we cannot understand:

To our master and patron, [So-and-So], from [several signatories and] all the people of the village of Euhemeria. We wish you to know, Lord, that even in your father's day, as under Your Beneficence, we have never handed over our bodies—rather, year in and year out, that we have completed our due services but surrender ourselves to no one. There is no stranger in our village, and there are two watchtowers, so no one can ride or walk into the village [unobserved]. But if any [?] should come for the best of our young fellows, we would not say you nay. Do whatever seems best to you to do.[51]

Our three texts give us snatches of conversation overheard in the country. They allow us to sense a range of tones, from the triumphant one of a man who rose above the humblest beginnings, to the servile and despairing address of peasants in a "monopolized" village. It is not easy to say much about the relationships implied, for they varied not only according to individual character but to time and place. Still, we feel always the great distance lying between master and man, patron and dependent.

How should the client-tenant seek a word with a "man of the arm," "the powerful," as he would be called?

He does not barge in on him abruptly, but comes, stands outside his gateway, and tells the servant, "So-and-So is standing at the gate of your court. Perhaps you will permit him to enter." [52]

On the two sides of the gate, two worlds: one with a dirt floor, one with a mosaic; one with debts, the other with property. They did not speak the same language—not in the metaphorical sense of the phrase, though that would be true enough, but often literally. Once away from his homeland in Greece or Italy, the Greek or Roman found himself among "people divided from us by language" (as John Chrysostom calls them), conquered by his forefathers and subjected to another civilization without easily becoming a part of it.[53] In cities and in the pieces of cities broken off—rich rural villas—he would be understood. Once outside, however, a thickening accent gradually gave way, mile by mile, to a total ignorance of the master tongues. In their stead, Aramaic, Phrygian, Arabic, Punic, Berber, Thracian. Egypt offers a specially clear illustration of the cultural gulf. An edict published from the capital in 215 announces:

> All Egyptians who are in Alexandria, and particularly the countryfolk who have fled from other parts and can easily be detected, are by all means to be expelled. . . . For the true Egyptians can easily be recognized among the linen weavers by their speech, which proves them to have assumed the appearance and dress of another class; moreover, their mode of life, their far-from-civilized manners, reveal them to be Egyptian countryfolk.[54]

And a writer who had been living in the country for a while wrote mock-apologetically to his friends in the metropolis, "You are perhaps thinking me a barbarian or an inhuman Egyptian." [55] In the face of such extreme prejudice, small wonder that marriages between the Greco-Roman ruling class and the despised Copts or Egyptians were frowned on by the law,[56] and so far as concerned the punishment of criminals, a cruel and invidious distinction was enforced:

> There are differences between scourges used in the city [of Alexandria], and these differences are regulated by the social standing of the persons to be beaten. The Egyptians are scourged with a different kind of lash and by a

different set of people, the Alexandrians with a flat blade,
and the persons who wield it are also Alexandrians.[57]

The burnous framing a sun-blackened face and shaggy
hair; the slow tongue, heavy step, and servile stupid address; the peasant's belief in strange gods and stranger
rustic spells—all these the city man tried to keep at a distance. He divided the human race into "duly registered,
and country-dwelling." [58] For all his efforts, some drift
from villages to cities drew the two worlds together in
the earlier Empire, followed later by a reverse movement
of emigration to the country. Both washed over the cultural barriers we have been emphasizing.[59] Besides the
harvester of Mactar, other lucky or ambitious individuals
rose from a cottage to a townhouse: a municipal senator
of Sulmo, for example, "the first from Betifulus" (the
name of his village), as he boasts.[60] Though explicit proof
of such success stories is rare, indirect evidence suggests a
quite widespread phenomenon. People with native names,
or sons and daughters of natives, appear in the honor rolls
of many a provincial center, risen there surely from the
countryside and Romanized, or Hellenized, by nomenclature, language, aspirations, and municipal office. Many
a village surely honors in its chosen patron some home-
town boy who made good. And the reverse is striking,
too. Various incentives encouraged those who had lived in
a city to spend a part of the year or take up permanent
residence on their estates. They qualified for village office
(it was common to require real property for the rank),[61]
and acknowledged the honor of election by paying for a
new public bath, a portico, or the like.[62]

It is often said that urban wealth lay chiefly in rural holdings. The truth of the statement is amply confirmed by close study of particular cities.[63] It is often said, too, by the ancients themselves, that "of all the sources of wealth farming is the best, the most fruitful, the most agreeable, the most suited to a free man"—so Cicero, but Rabbi Eleazar too declares, Anyone who owns no land is no proper man.[64] In the face of such testimony, the great authority of Rostovtzeff supports a rather different view. He begins a crucial passage,

> No scholar has endeavored to collect the evidence about the rich men of the second century, about the sources of their income, and about the character of their economic activity. A careful investigation of this subject promises good results.

So far, agreed; but what he was pondering fifty years ago was really a most curious and central crux in Roman studies. A pity that, in the long interval since then, it has received no attention. It reduces to this fact, that plenty of evidence for wealth-producing activity in the empire exists, and plenty for concentrations of its yield in the hands of individuals; but very little evidence indeed for the ties between the two. For illustration: among thousands of inscriptions that detail the gifts made by patrons to guilds, cities, or other groups, only a tiny number indicate where the donor got his money.[65] Again, thousands of oil lamps made by one particular firm occur at sites widely scattered over the empire, without any indication of who the head of the firm was (we know the bare

name) or how much it brought in as income; hundreds
of prosperous villas have been excavated, without yielding
the name or occupation of the owner. And hundreds of
property transfers (mostly real estate) can be traced in
various ways, without our being able to say just how the
estates originally accumulated. The gap in knowledge must be filled somehow. Rostovtzeff continues:

> As far as I can judge from the evidence I have got to-
> gether, the main source of large fortunes, now [in the
> second century] as before, was commerce. Money acquired
> by commerce was increased by lending it out mostly on
> mortgage, and it was invested in land.[66]

Though he brings forward no really hard facts in support
of all this, it represents a wide consensus and is of course
much more than idle conjecture. It might be challenged
in another work, not of social history but of economic;
and we will touch on the question again (below, pp. 97 f.)
when we come to social mobility. But it cannot be completely neglected here, where we are dealing with the
relations between the rural and urban populations. It is
my view that land was by far the preponderant ultimate ✓
producer of wealth and that it and the cities in its midst
were thus closely symbiotic.

A well-known illustration used by Rostovtzeff and by
others of a like opinion is Trimalchio. Trimalchio—a fiction, to be sure—was meant by his creator to embody
everything contemptible in the nouveau riche. For that
very reason he must surely typify what an observer of

first-century Italy felt to be a likely career. It began with his being bought as a slave boy. "Master's pet, for fourteen years. No disgrace, if it's the master who made me—and I kept the mistress happy, too. You know what I mean." [67] His obliging role resulted in his being named sole legatee of an estate wholly in lands and cash, part of which he diverted to experiments in commerce—at first with disastrous loss, then with an equal success. Thus much and no more for the Rostovtzeffian idea of how to get rich. For thereafter Trimalchio entrusted his profits to loans and real estate (some urban, the vast majority agricultural). [68] His was no passive retirement. Wealth built up through rents and interest. All his accounts were well kept, his land worked for him, and he and his friends still called themselves businessmen even while drawing their income from arable or vineyards. [69]

His investments reflected the prevailing wisdom of capitalists of the time. Pompeii and its environs allow us to apply a unique test of archeology to a figure of fiction. The two fit perfectly. "Wine growers . . . were members of the most wealthy and prominent families in Pompeii. In fact, they represent the governing aristocracy of the city." [70] Theirs are the grandest townhouses and suburban villas, on whose walls are painted artistic tributes to the profits that Bacchus brings; their families (for example, in the election of 69/70) supply half the candidates for municipal office. Fortunes like theirs stir that agricultural expert of the time, Columella, to declare, Wine pays best, and the elder Pliny to pick out for comment the enormous "killings" made in viticulture. [71] Casting our net wider, we find men whom we know to be rich, in Italy and the provinces, combining wine production with cereal production or with cattle;[72] sometimes, the latter alone. "Whoever wants to become wealthy should engage in the breeding of small cattle," meaning goats and sheep. The advice serves as a rabbi's comment on the great expanses of pasture in Greece, Italy, or western Asia Minor.[73]

But to return to Trimalchio as the model and to his disposition of his funds partly in land, partly in loans: Dio Chrysostom, like his father before him, relied on both; Apuleius speaks offhand of "wealth in lands and loans," as of a stock situation; Herodes Atticus had vast scattered holdings in Greece and equal amounts out at interest; Horace, Martial, Pliny, and Seneca take wealth by definition to mean "rich in fields, rich in money out at interest"; and litigation as reflected in the Digest assumes the same pairing.[74] When Jesus wants to portray a typical rich man, he chooses one with loans due him of thousands of denarii, a thousand gallons of olive oil, a thousand bushels of wheat.[75] His parables round out a first- and second-century survey of Judaea, Bithynia, Africa, Greece, and Italy, along with the remarks of contemporaries intended to apply to all regions generally. Our witnesses either speak unguardedly out of their everyday experience or as specific and undeniable instances of how investments were actually handled. In either case, they seem quite trustworthy. For money made in commerce no such texts can be named.

Debts payable in agricultural produce clearly point to debtors who are farmers. They recall the indebted laborers so common in Asia, Egypt, and Illyricum (above, page 34), adrift because they had lost their land given in surety for what they borrowed. In contrast, only as a rash and unusual practice would a man lend without demanding security in the form of property, "trusting in his own influence that no one would argue," i.e. try to default.[76] Mortagage, then, was as Rostovtzeff says the ordinary form of loan, yielding either fields foreclosed or interest in the neighborhood of 6–8 percent. The rate compared favorably with the 6 percent (at least in Italy) that one might reasonably hope for from money invested in agriculture.[77] At that, one's money doubled in a dozen years. Why take a chance in trade? Or if you had a gambler's spirit, you might still stay in farming and await a rise in prices. They fluctuated sharply and often;[78] and the "Haves" were ruthless in a time of shortage (above, p. 33).

Rostovtzeff, in passages far better known than those just discussed, sees the oppressed countryfolk in the third century taking their revenge on the urban population. As conscripts to an army pampered and indulged in acts of rapacity, the peasants waged a sort of class war on "the cities of the empire, their chief enemies."[79] Though Rostovtzeff's vision of that troubled century is not generally shared by other scholars, it has a certain plausibility, derived not so much from the material that he thought supported it as from a broader argument of motivation. Peasants certainly had reason to revolt. Consider the seizing of their stocks of food by profiteers in the very heart of famines and the wretched substitutes they had to fall back on; their deprivation even in good years, shown by their crowded housing, short life expectancy, exposure of children, and bitter disputes over the use of land and water; their indebtedness, while urban prosperity unfolded column-lined streets, public bath buildings, and private palaces. From that luxurious life they were shut out by what seemed an alien race of masters who dressed, spoke, dined, and thought in a distinctive and exclusive way, and appeared in the rural districts chiefly as exploiters.

At two junctures in the empire's history, indeed, rural-urban relations do seem to break down into actual warfare; once, around the middle of the first century in Judaea, a second time in Africa two hundred years later.[80] This may not be the place to study the story of the Zealots and the Circumcellions; but plainly peasants under the name and banner of religious fanatics dared to take up arms against the wealthy and inflicted a bloody revenge on those from whom, in normal times, they went cap in hand to borrow money or seed corn.

But the argument based on motivation trips over the word "normal." Fair enough, to emphasize the polarity so often sensed between "men of the arm" and *obaerarii*. The two semitechnical terms (above, pp. 42, 34) are representative of a range of hostile acts and customs. The very weakness of the peasant, however, prevented violent outbreaks from being anything but abnormal. And Zealots and Circumcellions must be balanced against other figures typifying a quite different side of the relationship: the Mactar harvester rising into the ranks of the urban aristocracy, or still another farmer who made it into town—on a

mule. A gravestone that survives shows us a certain Lucius
Calidius Eroticus in the act of paying his bill at a Pompeian inn. He has journeyed in for a day of business, a
flagon of wine before retiring, and a girl for the night.
Now, in the funerary relief, he has put on his hooded
cloak that countrymen wore and gets ready for the ride
home.[81]

The snapshot of this little moment, printed on stone, is
evidence for the peaceful dependence of the rural population on urban centers. By no other means could farmers
so easily find a market for their surplus and the special
goods and services even their simple needs required. Exchange was daily.

> The peasants must have not too long a journey to bring
> their produce to the city. It is desirable, even, that they
> should be able to make the round trip in one day; three
> or four hours' walk is the maximum. They leave before
> dawn for the city, their donkeys laden with cereals, olives,
> grapes, or figs, depending on the season. Towards seven
> or eight o'clock the bazaar is full; souks and khans bulge
> with goods, animals, and people. Towards ten o'clock,
> time to think of one's own purchases—the few items of
> luxury which the land does not yield: cloth bought in the
> city ever since rural production died, salt, sugar, soap, oil
> for the evenings. Towards eleven, the city is emptied and
> everyone starts home.[82]

The description of this human ebb and flow into a modern
Syrian town needs the change of only a word or two to
fit whatever we know of Roman times.

Material needs were often paired with spiritual. Great

holy days drew great crowds—a momentary market like
a medieval fair ideal for buyer and seller alike. Booths
were set up in the very precincts of the temples.[83] There
the peasant could sacrifice, pray, price the wares, and
gawp at the throngs, thereafter moving on, perhaps, to
a horse race or gladiatorial combat (for such spectacles
were usually timed to coincide with religious festivals).
In several cities—Carnuntum, Lambaesis, Seleucia in Cili-
cia—he would even find a section of amphitheater seats
reserved for the people of his particular village, surely
the most honorific welcome any *paganus* could ask for.[84]

Town and country got along together, then, because
they had to. Very different their needs, very unequal their
resources, and of course very different their treatment of
each other. If in the relationship the peasant seems most
often the loser, that was simply his lot, to give and suffer,
but to get something in return as well.

No monument serves better to dramatize this relationship than the amphitheater at El-Djem, in southern Tunisia; nothing prepares the traveler for its revelation. Set
back behind a scattering of a few twisting streets of one-
or two-story whitewashed houses in an altogether unimpressive little town, it soars a hundred feet and more into
the air. Sixty thousand spectators could be seated in it.
What paid for it, in a land now semidesert? The answer,
oil. For miles around, in Roman times, grew vast olive
orchards, with cereal crops in furrows between the rows
of trees, requiring the labor of a population of tenant
farmers and laborers ten times what the region would support today. Landlords, their names now unknown, grew

rich from the yield and built the amphitheater as a gift
for a town in which the citizens—men, women, and children—nowhere near sufficed to fill the seats. The seats
were filled, however—by the countryfolk streaming in on
festival days to stare, laugh, clap, and shriek at vastly expensive shows put on for free by the very landlords that
exploited their labors in the sun.

III

URBAN

The area of our study held two swollen giants of cities, Alexandria and the capital itself, both containing over - half a million inhabitants. It held two other near-giants, Carthage and Antioch; perhaps a half-dozen others with more than seventy-five thousand; the rest, much smaller. Pompeii's twenty thousands were typical. One could fairly call oneself a city-dweller and still be overwhelmed by the sheer size of Rome. On the other hand, the architectural elements and the activities they implied were strikingly similar wherever one went: open centers still called marketplaces though with very diverse functions; theaters and amphitheaters; baths and exercise halls; temples, basilicas, senate houses, ornamental fountains, porticoes lining the chief avenues, and such minor buildings as public latrines and jails. All these things in an expense-be-damned fashion expressed the highest ambitions of imperial civilization.

Citizens of the capital felt themselves vastly superior to men of any other origin. Tacitus lists "among so many sorrows that saddened the city" in the year 33 the marriage of a woman of the royal family to someone "whose grandfather many remembered as a gentleman outside the senate, from Tivoli" [1]—the horror of the mésalliance lying no more in equestrian rank than in the stain of small-town birth a bare two generations ago. If we ask who "the city" is that felt such grief, and who "the many" are who reckoned up the inadequate years since immigration to Rome, we lay bare an almost incredible snobbery. For Tacitus, in certain respects an utter fool, only the few thousands of his own circle really existed. Two centuries later, however, Ammianus met his like in Rome—"Some men of ridiculous vanity count as worthless everything that originates outside the city's bounds" [2]—while Cicero, two centuries earlier, complained, "You see how all of us are looked down on who come from country towns." [3] Cicero nevertheless goes on to say, "You might think [one] was speaking of a person from Tralles or Ephesus." Scorn of those provincial cities was after all quite understandable. And in private he writes to a friend, "You can see all the slapstick you want in your Pompeian senate meetings." [4] The Greeks naturally had a word for what he found so absurd: micropolitics.[5]

They had another word, *asteios,* literally "urban" but by extension "fine," "refined," "good" in general,[6] recalling but going beyond our "urbane." We saw at the outset of the preceding chapter how that quality triumphed in contrast with everything nonurban, i.e. rustic. But if everything about any city was good, then the bigger the city the better. The Nicomedians, a contemporary reports, "are very proud of their larger population" than Nicaea's [7] —just because it *was* larger. Similarly, cities asserted the claim and attached to themselves the title "Greatest", or quarreled over whose temple to Zeus or whose amphitheater was the bigger.

Reasons of status as much as anything else underlay the narrow exclusiveness that characterized the formal definition of citizenship. In official documents we often encounter the terms arranged in a significant series: Citizens, Residents (but not owning real property), Transients (or Businessmen), and those Outside the Walls (or Rural).[8] The defining agent was the municipal charter backed by the imperial government. What concerns us here is neither the language nor the legal niceties but rather the implications for common behavior; and it is unfortunate that we can so rarely go beyond the obvious inference that those who were not citizens could not vote. At Tarsus in the second century, the rights of one group came into question—"a group of no small size, outside the constitution, so to speak, whom some people call 'linen-workers' and are irritated by them and consider them a useless rabble and the cause of uproar and disorder." Though for the most part native-born and admitted to the assembly, they were yet "reviled and viewed as aliens." [9] This mention, almost unique in putting a little flesh on the bare bones of terminology, recalls the weavers in Alexandria as a separate, tolerated, but somehow still foreign element in the population. We may add "the artisans" excluded from the franchise at a city in Greece, Messene;[10] and there is a match, too, for the accusation by Tarsus' city fathers that aliens were to blame for any local unrest (outside agitators, they would be called nowadays). In this very fashion Cicero will never admit that true Romans, who to a man wished him well, could have supported his enemies; neither could Libanius imagine that his beloved Antiochenes had acted up.[11] The feelings of both Cicero and Libanius are quite understandable. They shrank from facing a rift or failure in their society. On the other hand, of course, the very exclusiveness of their society marked out with varying degrees of explicitness people who enjoyed no rights in the community but who could still enter it freely. They broke its rules far less than we would expect.

Except for a footnote to be added later (p. 83) on immigrant enclaves, we really know next to nothing about the attitudes to be sensed among noncitizens. In contrast, the loyalty aglow among the urban insiders is one of the best known and historically important aspects of both Greek and Roman antiquity. They often give expression to it: in the boast scribbled on the wall of a Campanian tavern by a customer from abroad, "Pergamum, golden city," below which another competitively patriotic hand has added, "Rome, golden city"; or again,

Let the traveler across thy lands, most holy Mustis,
Pluck up strength of mind and body, seeing thy varied scene

—so runs the couplet inscribed on some public building in a city of Africa Proconsularis.[12] Hear the words of Prusa's leading orator, quoting Homer—"For naught is sweeter than one's native land"—and somewhat circumspectly proclaiming Prusa "not the largest of cities nor the earliest settled, but more honored than many others, even by men of other cities [the ultimate tribute]; and its own citizens, contending with very nearly all Greeks, it has long placed not among the last, nor third, nor second rank." [13] We can imagine what applause that boast received. The masses who heard it were uplifted from their penurious anonymity to a proud height, while the rich credited themselves with the splendor of thronged streets and marble buildings. Rich and poor alike loved the object that gave them standing in the world.

They could not offer their lives for it; there was no call, no war; so those who could gave their wealth, with a generosity unequaled in any other period of human history. The aristocracy gave not in the form of unavoidable tax payments but through perfectly free donations of time, in unsalaried magistracies, or embassies, or court duty, or more directly through sums of money quite out of proportion to their means. Their readiness to mortgage their estates or anticipate their income for years to come can be inferred from the size of their gifts, the achievements of which survive to us only as ruins, to be sure, but ruins of extraordinary magnificence. The physical magnificence of imperial civilization rested ultimately on sheer willingness.

To explain this willingness carries us into the realm of speculation; but speculation need not carry us beyond common sense and common feeling. Two factors to take account of have already been noticed, exclusiveness and status. People used the first to emphasize the second. They competitively asserted their status against the patriots of neighboring cities through the acknowledged claims of material amenities—a grander temple, a grander amphitheater. And competition for status, exclusively asserted through an honorific title or one's name spread over the entrance of a building, operated on individuals just as on an entire community. "Most people," says Plutarch, "think that to be deprived of the chance to display their wealth is to be deprived of wealth itself." [14] It was the thirst for honor, the contest for applause, that worked so powerfully to impoverish the rich.

The verticality and show that characterized the empire's social structure made status conspicuous. Conspicuous, too, were the means of advertising one's claims to particular honor for some particular service. Lengthy tests recording a generous gift for all eternity unroll across many thousands of surviving stones. What most magnified honor, however, was the degree to which city life was lived publicly, in the open. Thus, whatever one was or did, everybody knew at once.

They knew because the vast majority spent so much time out of doors. The wealthy in their big houses had no need for that; but space occupied by *rus in urbe,* by pleasure-, vegetable-, and flower-gardens, by peristyles, stables, private baths, and vast reception halls, was space taken from the less fortunate,[15] whose very different lot we can best appreciate by a comparison between ancient and modern densities of urban population. That of Roman

times approached two hundred per acre, significantly
higher than the range we are used to,[16] and moreover distributed much less evenly over the whole city. Public areas
in the cities of the empire took up a fourth of the land,[17]
counting temples, fora, amphitheaters, streets, market
buildings, senate house, basilicas, sports parks, gymnasia,
and baths. So much the less for private housing. No doubt
great variations appeared in the whole long list of urban
centers; as Polybius said, the historian cannot reconstruct
the whole world of the past "by visiting every notable
city, one by one, and certainly not by looking at separate
plans of each one"; [18] but if it is our aim to speak at least
in general terms of our subject, we can assert as certain
that the bulk of the population had typically to put up
with most uncomfortable crowding at home, made toler-
able by the attractive spaciousness of public facilities.

To return, then, to the conclusions that follow from the
distribution of living space: the narrower one's house, the
more time would naturally be spent among one's neighbors, the more intercourse and friendliness, the more
gossip and exchange of news and sense of fraternity. The
merest glance at a plan of Ostia or Lepcis Magna suggests
patterns quite alien to our own experience—patterns evi-
dent to the mind's eye, without considering in detail the
meaning of a temple, a palaestra, an amphitheater. Of
course such buildings imply specific types of meetings at
specific times of the day or of the year. We need not dwell
on such familiar features of Roman imperial culture. It is
clear, however, that even in the little alleys a vibrant sense
of community joined the inhabitants, leaning on their

window-sills to see the sights and talk with each other
from apartment to apartment, while, lacking room at
home, the flayer below stripped the hide off a carcass on
the sidewalk, the teacher taught his circle of pupils their
ABCs, the notary or scribe drew up a rental contract at
his table, the barber shaved his customers, the clothes-
cleaner hung garments out to dry, the butcher cut up
meat. Rarely they asked official permission. After all, was
it not *their* city? [19]

Among these crowds itinerant vendors hawked their
wares—articles of clothing, hot sausages and pastries, or
whatever—each kind of peddler with his own cry.[20] The
general noisiness of the streets caused angry complaint.
A particular target might be the quarreling of loungers
over dice; another, the indecent songs that rose from the
harbor.[21] The loungers were undeterred, even had the impudence to carve their dicing boards on the broad flagstones of the forum, or passed the day over their game and
a single drink at the sidewalk table of a restaurant.[22] The
street was their livingroom, as for the restaurant-owner it
served as an extension of his business premisses. In that
sense, then, everyone spent his day at work or play in his
neighbor's house.

In consequence, little privacy: any kind of rumpus
brought a crowd.[23] Litigation took on the quality of a
family quarrel, for everyone knew the litigants, liked or
disliked them, and could assess the probability that one or
the other might be capable of crime. At this point, after a
digression on the common man's use of space in the city,
we return to our earlier concern with the publicness of

life. The law took formal advantage of the fact that one's
general character would be familiar to those around him.
In certain unusual situations, this might not be true. With
the innkeeper where one stayed the night or the captain
of a ship just anchored, special rules of conduct came to
bear.[24] Otherwise one knew perfectly well what sort of
person he was dealing with and could in that knowledge
safely bind himself to a verbal agreement. "Stipulation,"
as it was called in Roman law, dispensed with writing
yet remained in universal and constant use.[25] A personal
promise that committed one's community standing to a
bargain, it prevailed even where a different kind of security might have been expected, in the business world; but
Romans preferred men's word to their property, their
pledge to their deposit. The cement of their daily financial
relationships was people, not things.[26]

Disputes could be settled by simple assertion under oath,
challenging one's opponent to swear in turn;[27] a debt
could be proved simply by the entry made in one's
books;[28] and though the warning, "Let the buyer beware," we owe to the Romans (who certainly took for
granted that buying and selling was a game of wits), yet
for a businessman it was money in the bank to be known
as honest.[29]

Like the readiness of the rich to adorn their city, the
ability of plain people to deal with each other in directly
personal terms required that they be acquainted with each
other, that their doings and reputation be a matter of
common report. Such complex institutions as liturgy and
law thus rested on simple things: the warmth of the Medi-

terranean, for one, which allowed open-air life. But the picture should not become too idyllic. The poverty of the soil was another simple thing, too, and the fight for wealth in a society based ultimately on agriculture. Losers, being crowded into cramped quarters, gladly spent the daylight hours outdoors.

Mention of poverty, crowding, and litigation prepares us for the darker side of urban relationships. Someone who hoarded grain in time of shortage or brought defilement in the eyes of the gods or in any way attacked the whole community risked mob violence. People would pick up anything that lay in the street—cobbles, broken tiles, rocks—and let fly. Stoning, actual or threatened, stains the history of all the chief cities of the empire and a chance scattering of the minor ones.[30] It was a common form of group vengeance. Children learned it at play.[31] If it availed nothing against a powerful citizen in a strong house, the mob tried arson.[32] Per contra, if one was threatened with violence he could yell for help; crowds offered protection against criminal attack, neighbors and servants against a personal enemy.[33] The same patterns of interdependence in the streets show in the anger of the city as in its other moods.

In time of real need, appeal to the city at large did no good. Closer ties of neighborhood had to be called on. When the aristocracy spoke along those lines, they meant their connections with a country-town or country district; rather, with their peers in these settings.[34] The average man had narrower horizons of friendship. Their study leads into the subdivisions of the city.

Physical features on occasion not only gave a name to
parts of the population, as the Upper Town-, Harbor-, or
Acropolis-Dwellers, but set them at odds with other parts
in fights and factions.[35] Such large groupings, however,
rarely aroused so much loyalty, perhaps because divisions
according to wealth were likewise rare. Class and locality
thus could not reinforce each other. A slum might be dis-
tinguishable in the minds of contemporaries, the better
drained and cooler, higher parts of urban terrain might be
monopolized by the houses of the rich;[36] but the evidence
for such sections adds up to little. Equally meaningless
in terms of people's feelings were the fourteen precincts
of the capital, the invention of Augustus, and the five al-
phabetical ones in Alexandria. Who after all would want
to lay down his life for Letter B? Unless coincident with
national origin—as with the Jews in their separate quarters or with immigrant colonists from Italy to a native
center in the provinces—urban divisions that embraced
many tens of thousands of inhabitants proved too large to
be meaningful.[37]

Certain voting units of intermediate size enjoyed the
prominence of assigned sections in the municipal amphitheater,[38] as well as one or another of the usual appur-
tenances of public status: communal property (a baths
building, a reunion hall), a youth organization engaging
its like in athletic contests, and priests and civil officers
and public banquets.[39] From these perquisites can be inferred the rewards of belonging. Members stood out
among the crowds at a gladiatorial spectacle, sitting in
the front rows. *Proedria,* as it was called, placed them in

the company of the town's most honored ranks.[40] And banquets joined in a body a whole range of associations, from the Roman senate to the smallest village, generally in an outdoor setting,[41] partly (we may guess) to show everybody just who was included and who excluded. In the open community of the ancient city, fellowship was no more agreeable than the envy that well-advertised privileges aroused among one's neighbors.

In fact, however, the fellowship of some voting tribes— one sixth of the whole population of Laodicea, a fifth of Ephesus, a half of Samos—involved almost too large a membership to hold much significance.[42] Only when a subdivision marks out no more than two or three hundred people does it arouse intensity of feeling. That would be the case among the more numerous voting units of moderate-sized cities. In one such, a rule gives us an illustration. It obliges all members from within a six-mile circuit to attend a comrade's funeral. That was a long walk for loyalty's sake.[43]

Principally in Italy and best known in Rome, street associations (*vici*) demonstrated a special vitality, well attested in the sources. When Cicero describes how agitators set about collecting a mob, it is "street by street"; when Caesar organizes a census, it is by the same method; and when Augustus tries to infuse some order and support for his regime into the population, he does so through the formal recognition of 265 *vici* (let us say, five hundred adult males to each) whom he banqueted at state expense and encouraged in the offering of prayer to the capital's divine protectors through cross-roads cults (*compitalia*).[44]

At *compitalia* the youths of the street competed in games
under the direction of the *magistri vicorum,* whose annual choice by lot from the freedmen residents Augustus
had arranged in hopes of meshing this class into the
machinery of his administration.[45] Street associations
went back a long time, maybe as far back as the days of
the kings. The little niches at streetcorners for the worship of the protective *lares* were long familiar, and the
adding of the names of the year's *magistri* to the corner
walls or over the public fountain[46] fitted naturally into
the scene. A sense if participation animated the whole.
So, where municipal elections continued, elsewhere than
at Rome, it was *vicini* who could be counted on to lend
vociferous support to the candidate living in their midst.[47]

With the religious, political, and social ties that made a
community out of a mere physical collection of houses,
the economic combined. While most streets took their
names from prominent buildings or monuments nearby,
or from some person honored in the neighborhood long
ago, quite a number were called Glass, Incense, or Perfume Street, because of the concentration there of trade in
those commodities. Other common terms for locality—
square, plaza, portal, marketplace—bore similar prefixes:
Jewelers', Wainwrights', Vintners', Cobblers', Muleteers',
in urban centers of every province. The prefix could stand
alone. If you asked a man where he lived, he might reply,
Among the barbers.[48] The very abundant texts of these
kinds are proof of a ubiquitous and most important fea-
ture of urban life, the specializing of particular areas in
particular economic activities. To inscriptions that record

place-names we may add, first, the references in ancient literature showing that residents of Rome knew exactly where to go to buy dyes, honey-salve, books, clothes, or jewelry.[49] Second, we may add archeological data, much of it from the better-excavated European provinces but enough from Italy, too, to show that identifiable quarters for one or another industry characterize our own region of study: for instance, the tanners near the Stabian Gate at Pompeii, with a similar concentration of other workers near other gates; dyers, fullers, and combers along the midsection of the Via dell'Abbondanza; and the woolworkers generally confined to the suburbs of north Italian cities, where the commodity was produced in famous quality and quantity.[50] Third, we may turn to inscriptions that link a craftsman or tradesman with a given address.

City-dwellers in surprising number specify on their tombstones both their occupation and the place where they pursue it, in the form "So-and-So, butcher on the Viminal." To both connected facts about themselves they evidently attached great value. Only Rome's inscriptions allow a picture to emerge of clusters of engravers, gem-cutters, goldsmiths, and jewelers in one section, tailors and clothing-sellers in another, both toward the centers of commerce,[51] while other occupations more naturally gathered near the city's gates—traders or drovers—and porters near a municipal weighing station or point of debarkation.[52] All this we would expect to find, of course. It is also predictable that noxious industries would end up in the suburbs, since otherwise they aroused complaint about their smoke or smell. The Potters' Quarter of Athens had many analogies elsewhere; smithies and tan-

neries that made plentiful use of urine were notoriously
bad neighbors.[53] Since tombs were likewise exiled beyond
the city, being both religiously and physically unclean,
embalmers and tomb guards had to live apart as (in the
Greek term) "the folk beyond the gates."[54] A consistent
scale of values emerges, matching cultural and social prej-
udices with the place of one's residence or work. The
closer to the heart of the city, the more respectable; the
farther away, the more scorned, until the suburbs melted
into the countryside.

The clustering together of fellow-craftsmen seems
easily explained by reasons of pure convenience. A spectacular illustration offers us the makers of so-called Arretine pottery in a sort of great compound in southern
France; within our own area of study, a rabbi speaks of a
place in Palestine where "most of the inhabitants are engaged in dyeing";[55] Strabo tells us of another little town
wholly given over to fishing, and a host of products were
sold in antiquity as being genuinely from this or that
famous point of manufacture.[56] Moving toward the present, a point of concentration such as Rome's Clivus Argentarius has as its kin the Ponte Vecchio in Florence, the
Vicolo degli Orefici in Siena, and the Quai des Orfèvres
in Paris. If someone were to attempt for urban sociology
the same very loose generalizing that I sketched in my
discussion of villages, it might well appear that the shape
of medieval Mediterranean cities bore many of the same
traits as those to be found in Roman imperial times, including not only the organization of trades by quarters
but other features that belong to this chapter.[57]

But precisely what convenience drew tradesmen together? Industries needing large supplies of clay, fuel, or water are easily understood. So, too, those services—of inns, drovers, or porters—that naturally offered themselves at points of entry to the city. What, however, could produce a street full of booksellers? What was it about ancient commerce that imposed such a pattern?

The answer lies in the attempt of both buyer and seller to find each other. Everyday necessities, presenting no difficulties in this regard, appeared for sale promiscuously on every street; every street supplied sufficient customers to support at least a small business. That was true of food shops, for instance, which might reach out to a wider market by peddling their wares from door to door.[58] Goods in bulk or expensive items in rare demand were ingeniously handled by a pair of specialists, the *coactor* who served as broker and the *praeco* or crier who advertised whatever was for sale.[59] But articles of trade falling between the two extremes of cheapness and expense, between common demand or uncommon—that is, things like shoes, coats, perfume, incense, bracelets, books, wagon-wheels, scythes, or furniture—naturally ended up at a spot where, as everybody would know, just those items could be sold. The buyer for his part applied the same knowledge to seek out the right quarter of the city, there to shop around among the many competing merchants. They should not be pictured in the past, any more than in many nonwestern cities today, as competing very keenly; at any rate, nothing suggests a struggle to get one's share of the market. Quite to the contrary, a great deal suggests that a friendly, gossipy atmosphere prevailed among people who saw each other every day, worked at the same job in the same neighborhood, and shared all the same ups and downs. Trade associations were the result.

Under a score of different titles, some of which will be considered in a moment, trade associations sprang up in every city of any size and in a large number where one would hardly expect to find population sufficient for a respectable membership. They enrolled anywhere from a dozen to one or two thousand—typically, above a hundred—getting their start historically in Italy but spreading with greater and greater popularity into the Greek-speaking provinces, so that, by the middle of our period, their presence in a town can reasonably be assumed even if it happens not to be directly proven. Around their point of origin they most often united various branches of the building trade; toward the east, trades connected with the several stages of the garment industry predominate; but a random list of examples drawn from the standard books on the subject will contain a revealing and remarkable cross section of the ancient economy: sailors, pilots, bargees, divers, longshoremen, caulkers, shipwrights, cordwainers; joiners, inlayers, ebonists, cabinetmakers, sawyers, millhands, coopers, carpenters; mosaicists, fresco-painters, floor-layers, plasterers; cleaners, weavers, dyers, clothiers, ragpickers, bag-makers, tailors, felterers; tanners, cobblers, bootmakers, hosiers; farriers, bronze-, silver-, gold-, iron-, and nail-smiths; dancers, tragedians, comedians, singers, flutists, harpists, choristers, and many, many other specialists quite untranslatably named according to what they did for a living.[60]

For our purposes it is enough to glance quickly at trade

and crafts associations under the heading of their public role, first, and then under the heading of their social activities.

It fits with the growth of associations in localities that they might take in an occasional person who qualified only by residence, not by his craft; but they were generally entitled to call themselves with more or less truth and more or less claim to inclusiveness "The Poulterers," "The Bakers," and sometimes "The Crafts-Fellowship of . . . ," or "The Entire Craft of. . . ." [61] Such titles, applied to groups in cities as in villages (above, p. 17), invite a false analogy with modern labor unions. Crafts associations do indeed act as a larger, more influential whole to protect their economic interests. A familiar case is the protest raised by the Artemis-imagemakers at Ephesus against St. Paul's proclaiming of a new God; less familiar, the choosing of a guild's patron from among the ranks of government officials directly connected with its daily business. An occasional inscription needs only the change of a word or two to match what was engraved on a piece of English presentation silver: [62]

> Presented in grateful tribute to Thos. Ainsworth Esq., Bolton-le Moors, by the Bleachers, Dyers and Printers of the county of Lancaster, for his prompt and assiduous attention to their interests in obtaining the drawback of the Duties upon Salt used in the process of bleaching. June 29th, 1807

In the same fashion, a well-known and, as we will see, an almost public group of a hundred Roman bleachers could apply pressure to a town official that the same hundred as individuals could never dream of. United, they could invoke the unwritten rules that governed the obligations of a patron, to yield to the interests of his clients or intervene in their behalf.

But what is striking about Roman crafts in operation is not that they pushed their interests as defined in a modern sense but that they did so only very rarely indeed. In a different, ancient sense they proved on the other hand as active as they were successful. Scholars agree on one thing: they find close to no evidence at all for strikes, control over entry to the craft, the maintaining of wages at artificial levels, the remission or lowering of payments for taxes, tolls, or licenses, or the securing of shorter working days and more frequent holidays. Instead, associations seek benefits unconnected with their work. They can command the patronage of really important persons, expressed through the most handsome gifts—of money, to be used for the recipients' normal doings and meetings; of whole buildings, like the sales-hall presented to the clothiers of Pompeii by the heiress Eumachia; [63] of honor, to be asserted on the strength of having at the head of their membership a constellation of names known and respected throughout the city. A slipper-cobbler in Rome could hardly claim attention from any member of the aristocracy by himself. Hundreds such were another story. Similarly with other humble artisans: in the next chapter we will consider their place on the social ladder more carefully, but there is no need to explain here that hucksters or small-time barkeeps enjoyed a certain standing in the community solely through their incorporation.[64] In that form, they might then see their festival days inserted in the city's official calendar, themselves given seats of their own in the municipal amphitheater, and their title inscribed on stone for their contributions to some civic improvement.[65] No one smiled at their pretensions when their banners paraded through the streets in homage to a god or emperor;[66] no one found their honorific decrees or their emphatically advertised votes of thanks, even to personages miles above them socially, in the least ridiculous.[67] Their political support was most acceptable to candidates for a magistracy at Pompeii or to much more significant figures who stood in the need of lobbyists.[68] The arrogation of fancy titles raised no laugh against the Sacred Craft of Linen-Workers, the Most August Work-Center of Wool-Washers, the Most August Union of Fishers, the Universal Sacred Consistory of Linen-Weavers, the Corporation of Most Noble Money-Changers, the Holy College of Dyers.[69] It followed that their internal organization should ape the high-sounding terminology of larger, municipal bodies, the nomenclature of officialdom, and honors like *proedria* and the award of gold crowns in their meetings. At least the larger craft associations constituted in every detail miniature cities.[70]

What is interesting about crafts associations for our purposes is the focusing of their energies on the pursuit of honor rather than of economic advantage. The latter they did not completely ignore, to be sure. Still, they cared a lot more about prestige, which the members as individuals could not ordinarily hope to gain but which, within a subdivision of their city, competing with their peers, they could deal out according to a more modest scale of attainments. Associations thus resembled the whole social context they found themselves in and imitated it as best they could. Like everyone else, they sought status; and like the members of many other kinds of groups we have reviewed, they also sought a range of further satisfactions not felt or attainable in the undivided urban population.

If we turn next to their social activities, titles once again prove informative—titles like "The Friends and Construction-Workers," "Mates and Marble-Workers," "The Comrade Smiths" and "Brother Builders" [71]—while terms like *convivae* and *comestores* declared that the fellows shared their lives or, more commonly, their meals together.[72] For the purpose, they hired or quite often constructed at their own expense a set of rooms as a reunion hall. The Builders of Ravenna got permission to meet in the columned portico of the temple of Neptune; at Pompeii, the Porters, Youths, and Bleachers had their own halls, the Millers, Apple-Sellers, Gardeners, and Well-Diggers borrowed a corner café; in Tomi on the Black Sea, "The House" was simply another name for a local guild.[73]

What purpose did these places serve, among not only ✓ craftsmen but groups of all types? Pure comradeship. Friends liked to get together of an evening to eat, drink, and be merry. Moralists grumbled that they ate too much, to the point of inflating prices in the food markets; worse, that they drank too much, so that the associations common under the title "Fellow-Drinkers of . . . " were in reality organizations in the city in whose fellowship you could find no sound elements but only liquor, tippling, drunkenness and the outrageous conduct they lead to, associations and "couches" as they are called locally [in Alexandria]. In all or most of these religious associations Isidore reigned supreme, under the nickname Party Leader, Couch-Captain, or Master of the Rebels.[74]

For all the intent behind their gatherings, the riotous Isidore of our quotation seems to have had his like in associations of other types and places, whose rules and regulations "beg you all, comrades, to take your ease without ill-temper," to preserve "tranquility and propriety" and avoid hybris and abuse, "in common council to subscribe to the tie of friendship" and to appear on feast days "in your most decent clothes." [75]

A second-century constitution of an Italian association tells the story more fully.

On the fifth before the ides of June in the consulship of Lucius Ceionius Commodus and Sextus Vettulenus Civica Pompeianus [A.D. 136], in the township of Lanuvium in the temple of Antinous, the patron of the township Lucius Caesennius Rufus ordered a meeting to be called through Lucius Pompeius . . . censor of the Worshipers of Diana and Antinous. He promised . . . that from his generosity he would present them with 15,000 sesterces as endowment for the birthday of Diana on August 15th (in interest, 400 sesterces) and of Antinous on November 27th (in interest, 400 sesterces). . . . Those who wish to make their monthly contributions toward burial may enter this association, though, under guise of this association, they may not meet together more than once a month. . . . Whoever wishes to enter this association must contribute an initiation fee of 100 sesterces and an amphora of good wine. If anyone of this association shall die while in good standing, 300 sesterces shall be allotted from the treasury, from which sum for funeral expenses 50 sesterces shall be allotted to be divided up at his pyre; and the funeral procession shall proceed on foot.

Whoever in his year of office serves as president according to rotation in the membership list, for the giving of dinners, and fails to observe this duty and do this, shall pay the treasury 30 sesterces. The order of the dinners shall be, on March 8th, on the birthday of Caesennius . . . , on November 27th, on the birthday of Antinous . . . , on August 13th . . . , 20th . . . , January 14th. . . . Presidents of dinners in rotation of membership, four in number, shall provide, each one, an amphora of good wine, loaves of bread (cost, 2 *asses*) for the number of persons in the association, four sardines [for each member], furnishings of the table, hot water, and waiters. . . . If anyone wishes to bring up any matter of complaint he shall do so in a business meeting, so that our dinners on the usual days may pass off serenely and joyfully. Whoever leaves his place to cause a disturbance shall be fined 4 sesterces; if he insults another or is disorderly, he shall be fined 12 sesterces.[76]

Those here assembled represent a particularly prevalent type of association, a burial-insurance group; for both Greeks and Romans regularly signalized funerals and anniversaries of decease by banquets, and associations of all ✓ kinds had a common place of burial for their members.

But if piety counted for much, conviviality counted for more.[77] In a setting as rich and well-furnished as the members could afford—and they sometimes surprise us with their luxury—like dined with like, drawn together by the sharing of neighborhood, social class, occupation, or simple congenialty. Martial met in the Poets' Clubhouse, the philosophers of a small town in Africa had their place reserved in the municipal baths.[78] Even the young met with the young and the old with the old.

In the forming of associations on the principle of age, the Greek East, long before it fell to the Romans, took the first steps; but the Romans by that time had already institutionalized the generation gap in a notorious fashion. They looked on this hoary aspect of their civilization with reverence, and when they extended their law and citizenship throughout the empire they likewise extended the ancient rights of the paterfamilias to punish even a grown son of any age for the crimes of disrespect or disobedience to his parents.[79] We can always expect to hear the growls of elders directed at the depravity, self-indulgence, and ill-manners of the young,[80] but we actually find a man in Cicero's day ordering the execution of his son, and a serious debate going on in the second century A.D. over the question, Should a private citizen assert his rights to social precedence over his son during the latter's tenure of office as a provincial governor? [81] A high state official in the maturity of his career, on the news of his dishonorable discharge, implored the emperor Augustus for mercy. *"What shall I tell my father?"* was his plea.[82] Incredible! But we have no way of testing whether the habits of mind represented in that question also prevailed among the less conservative, less aristocratic classes, or whether such habits could be found outside of Italy at all. In the Greek East, however, the official dividing of the male population into age groups receded into the darkest past and, in the forms developed in Athens, transmitted to later centuries the ephebate. This was a semimilitary organization of the late teens. Within the period of our study, it appears in conjunction with other age groups, too. Most cities of any size poured their upper-class children into the mold of the gymnasium, where, in physical facilities of great cost under the care of special trainers and with annual displays of various athletic and cultural accomplishments, the boys ripened into ephebes, the ephebes into youths, and the youths into their forties, fifties, and sixties. As Elders, though they continued their exercises, they constituted more appropriately a separate, influential club called the *Gerousia*. While many details about the four stages of life remain obscure, they are well known in eastern provinces and less prominently in Italy and Africa. Occasionally the young and old are found at odds with each other in public quarrels; more often the young are accused of disorders on their own.[83]

We need only list the signs of status that distinguished one or another of these age associations in one or another place—*proedria,* reserved theater sections, mention in public documents, participation in acts of the community as a whole, or a share in largesses distributed to the population class by class from the hands of some public-spirited millionaire.[84] All honors resembled those enjoyed by

other groups we have discussed and can as fairly be used
to prove the satisfactions that membership conferred.
More curious, however, is the same principle of age turn-
ing up within smaller units than the whole male urban
population: as a subdivision of *vici,* for instance; in African municipal "tribes"; and within the general senatorial
stratum.[85] Most of the evidence is unadorned—a record on
stone that notes only in a series the town senators, married
women, and the children of the senatorial order.[86] It is as
if no principle of either inclusion or exclusion could meet
all demands—as if clusters of every conceivable private
sympathy required expression. Where two neighbors at a
corner pub today will raise their glasses and at most exchange a friendly "Cheers!" the two in antiquity seem to
have said, "Be it resolved, to call ourselves the society
of. . . ."

A *vicus* might contain a bit under a hundred members
(except at Rome), a crafts association a bit more (with a
wide range), a *gerousia* from seventy to a few hundred,
but a cult association only a few dozen.[87] This last-named
form underlay all the others, in a sense, for the assembled
Butchers, Youths, or whatever opened their meetings
with a prayer to the deity they had inevitably chosen at
the moment of their incorporation. On the other hand, it
is proper to single out as a distinct type the groups that
bear the name only of a god. In their choice of worship
we can sometimes detect a clue to one of the general
motives for incorporation. Just as certain crafts directed
their veneration to a god that specially favored their work
—wood-cutters to Silvanus of the forests, restaurateurs to

Bachus [88]—so aliens in a foreign setting picked out a divine patron that suited and sheltered their place of origin. The motive at work, for us to trace farther, is the loneliness felt by the newcomer to the city.

It is likely that the most popular worships had different rites in different places—that Italians in a Black Sea town would find the cult of their familiar Bacchus conducted in a strange way, so they would set up their own congregation.[89] They would be likely, too, to seek out more often than at home the deities especially sacred to their native city, for instance, Athena for Athenians abroad,[90] and to settle near the shrine of such a god transplanted to a foreign city. Thus the Egyptians in Rome settled around the temples of Isis and Serapis on the Campus Martius, the Syrians around the temple of Jupiter Dolichenus on the Aventine or Jupiter Heliopolitanus on the Janiculum.[91] Best known in the capital as in many other urban centers are the Jewish sections. If they grew large enough, they split up into separate congregations with separate synagogues, obeying however a common ghetto government and formally recognized as a state within a state by both the local municipal authorities and the Roman imperial.[92] To be the sole Jew in a street was a lonely business. Ritual isolated one from one's neighbors.[93] And Christians in the same way needed and got from each other special comfort through their comradely congregations.

Josephus tells us that the Essenes had communities widespread in Palestinian cities that would take in a wandering brother, clothe and feed and lodge him, and through a sort of chief welcomer minister to any need he might have.[94] At other cities, when one arrived from afar and had no friends or place to go, one could ask for the street or quarter where fellow-nationals lived and there receive a welcome from (let us instance) the Smyrna Union advertised in Magnesia, the Boeotian Community in Xois, the Lycian in Alexandria, and so forth.[95] The traveler might be a colonist sent by the state to a frontier town in the Danube provinces,[96] more likely a trader putting in at a port town. Puteoli provides in a long and famous inscription a

Letter written to the city of Tyre, the sacred, inviolable and autonomous metropolis of Phoenicia and of other cities, and mistress of a fleet. To the chief magistrates, council, and people of their sovereign native city, from the Tyrians resident in Puteoli, greeting.

By the grace of the gods and the good fortune of our lord the emperor, there is many a commercial agency in Puteoli, as most of you know, and ours excels the others both in adornment and in size. In the past this was cared for by the Tyrians resident in Puteoli, who were numerous and wealthy; but now this care has devolved on us, who are few in number, and since we pay the expenses for the sacrifices and services to our ancestral gods consecrated here in temples, we do not have the means to pay the agency's annual rent of 250 denarii, especially as the expenses of the Puteoli Ox-Sacrifice Games have in addition been imposed on us. We therefore beg you to provide for the agency's continued existence. And it will continue if you make the 250 denarii paid annually for rent your concern; for the remaining expenses, including those in-

curred to refurbish the agency for the birthday festival of
our lord the emperor, we set down to our own account, so
as not to burden the city. And we remind you that the
agency here—unlike the one in the capital, Rome—derives
no income either from shipowners or from merchants. We
therefore appeal to you and beg you to make provision for
this unfortunate circumstance. Written in Puteoli, July 23
[A.D. 174].[97]

Similar agencies of many cities and nations had their little
bureaus in Rome and Ostia,[98] where a stranger could at
least make his first social and business contacts; and the
Shippers and Merchants abroad—from Rome, from
Alexandria, from Malaca—organized themselves in the
kind of trade association we have already reviewed,
known at a host of sites.[99] The farther from home, the
more one felt one's nationality; the farther from home,
the more friendless; from both causes arose the typical
business-cult-locality associations of migrants.

The urban population also took in a steady tribute of
the poor from country districts round about. Some mention has been made earlier of the fellahin drawn to
Alexandria's weaving shops,[100] and Libanius speaks of the
escape that Antioch offered to the criminal and indigent.[101] They would squat in vacant lots or abandoned
buildings (for it is a mistake to imagine that no part of a
city in antiquity matched the state of decay that time has
left for the archeologist);[102] they would crowd into high
tenements that rose in at least a few Italian cities. Rich
people invested in such properties and lorded it over them
as they did over little villages on their estates. Owners

gave their name to entire blocks,[103] took the census of
their population, passed them on with their janitors to
their heirs, and when the buildings collapsed, thought
only of the financial loss involved. Cicero writes, in one
of his most unlovable letters,

> Two of my shops have fallen down and the rest are crack-
> ing; so not only the tenants but even the mice have mi-
> grated. Other people call it a calamity, but I don't even
> count it a nuisance. O Socrates and followers of Socrates,
> I can never thank you sufficiently! Ye gods!—how insig-
> nificant I count all such things. However, at the advice
> and on the suggestion of Vestorius I have adopted a plan
> of rebuilding which will make my loss a profit.[104]

But the urge to form little friendly societies and to think
of oneself as a part of a neighborhood, even if a vertical
one in some soaring apartment house, asserted itself ir-
repressibly. We have the record of a patron deity chosen,
its image set up, and prayers offered to it by the tenants of
the Bolan Building in Rome.[105]

For the poor, corner cafés served informally as clubs
(the cafés working out to about one for every fifty or
sixty adult males in Pompeii),[106] and more informally
still as houses of prostitution. They were forever being
shut down because of the noise, vice, and violence they
bred. Prostitution nevertheless flourished throughout the
cities of the empire, known to us chiefly through references to the taxes paid on the exercise of the profession.[107]
In the one place really well excavated, Pompeii, twenty-
eight brothels have been identified and, scattered along

back streets, another nine single rooms rented by prosti-
tutes.[108]

When these ill-starred women blinked out at the morning sun from their narrow quarters, they saw the beggar
sprawled still asleep in a patch of shade. No one paid him
much attention. "The poor you have among you always."
In the later Empire a pagan did pity "the mendicant poor,
covered with rags and sunk in the calamity of their
wretchedness," and a Christian reminded his listeners
that "the hand reached out to beg can be seen everywhere.
The open air is their dwelling, their lodgings are the
porticoes and streetcorners and the less frequented parts
of the marketplace." [109] These, however, are not mere
testimonies of Rome's decline. The problem was always
there for those who had eyes to see it. "Look you," said
Seneca, *"how great a majority are the poor."* [110] In Pompeii's marketplace they were enough (and felt themselves
not beneath the right of incorporation) to be called on for
a candidate's support. "The beggars demand his election,"
was written up on a wall above a long bench where the
city's poor sat the day through.[111]

IV

CLASS

The connection between money and standing that one ex-
pects to find in any society was (along with other, sometimes even more valued considerations) acknowledged by
the Romans from very early times. They found, wel-
comed, and generally made more explicit that connection
in other societies they conquered. For our present purposes, then—for the understanding of influence in the
community, the consequent sense of importance and dig-
nity and self-respect, one's hopes of attaining all these
things, and the manners that went with them—the distribution of wealth is a natural subject to begin with.

The population we are dealing with in the parts of the
empire lying between Sardinia and Syria approached
fifty millions in Tacitus' day (I choose a round number
lying between the indefensible extremes of mere conjecture). The senatorial stratum amounted to something like
two-thousandths of one percent (a figure that Tacitus

would have found deeply gratifying). *Equites* probably totalled less than a tenth of one percent. Senators had to have property worth 250,000 times the day's wage of a laborer; *equites* qualified for their rank by less than half of that estate. In Italy, at its richest moment, in its second largest city (Padua), the *equites* constituted no more than one percent of the inhabitants; in poorer regions of the empire and in the rural population of every region, *equites* were of course much scarcer.[1]

A scholar not long ago wrote a book on the *equites* called *The Roman Middle Class*. The absurdity of the title points to the difficulty experienced by our modern selves in coming to grips with a world utterly different from our own. We should guard against a blind insistence that there *must* be a middle class and that it must be sought where we are used to finding it today, in the urban commercial and industrial segments of the population. We should defend our estimates against the purely accidental survival of articles in stone, metal, and baked clay which distort the archeological record in the direction of nonexistent "factories"; and the very populousness of crafts associations should combine in our minds with other, perhaps less striking evidence for the subdividing of money-making opportunities into units too small to support a prosperous burgher.[2]

Statistically, there was indeed a middle class. Between the top and bottom, taking into account in a single glance the entire empire, a range of intermediate wealth made up the aristocracy of small cities. In a given city, however, the aristocracy nevertheless stood upon the summit of a very steep social pyramid. The feel of society, the living sense of its proportions, thus did not harmonize with statistics.

Big fish in small ponds went by a third term, to be defined, like *senatores* and *equites,* by the value of their landed property, generally farmland.[3] These were the decurions, municipal senators. Typically they numbered a hundred, in Italy and in the townships under the influence of Italian charters, whether colonies planted in the provinces or provincial centers that "went Roman." Eastern municipal senates varied in size from a membership of thirty up to five hundred. Decurions had to be rich (in Comum in Italy, property worth 25,000 denarii qualified, i.e. one-tenth of a Roman senator's minimum); consequently they were sometimes in short supply. Though Pompeii was no doubt prosperous enough to find the requisite number, other places had trouble: Tymandus, for one, requested a charter with a senate of only fifty, "urgently promising that there would be an adequate supply of decurions."[4] That meant only a tiny percentage of well-to-do, not vastly rich, citizens, and on the model of Comum implied assessed property to a total of no more than one and a quarter million denarii for its entire decurion class. The great majority of cities resembled Tymandus more than Pompeii, at least in size if not level of prosperity (for Tymandus' application came in a period of difficulties).[5] A second-century writer declares that "the whole city of Parium counting its five neighbors, and their men, livestock, and possessions together, would not fetch" thirty million denarii. His statement,

however loosely meant and whatever neighboring cities
he may have had in mind, sets the proportions for us
more truly than do the great centers like Pergamum,
Ephesus, Aquileia, or Jerusalem. And thirty millions for
six cities—that works out to five million each, only
enough for twenty Roman senators, fifty *equites,* or five
hundred municipal senators, always provided that no one
else had so much as a penny and that each member of the
defined ranks had no more than the minimum required.

Precise numbers in antiquity are too few to be used as
controls over each other yet by their rarity too precious to
ignore. Those we have chosen certainly suggest two
things: first, that an immense economic gulf separated
the senate of a large Italian city from that of a little town
in the provinces; second, that within each setting the
number of inhabitants who counted as rich was minute.
The resulting picture of urban aristocracies finds confirmation in the range of individual fortunes. While at Tymandus someone with one really big estate doubtless
stood out as a local magnate, to another city a benefactor
is recorded as giving two million denarii in a single act of
largesse.[6] Pliny over many years presented Comum with
fully half that sum, despite being (as he saw it) no bil-
lionaire. What lay behind his modesty was the prepon-
derance of the empire's wealth in the Roman homeland,
accumulated there during the Republic and during the
Empire concentrated into the hands of a narrowing nobility. Great Italian fortunes in Pliny's day towered above
all but a very few in the provinces. It does not of course
follow that he rated as middle class in the eyes of the men

whose wealth vastly exceeded his own, any more than he in turn would have counted as middle class the decurions of Tymandus. Terminology appropriate to our world simply does not fit the Roman.

At the bottom of the pyramid one might be tempted to place the slave population. In Italy it was enormous, possibly a quarter of the whole. In the provinces the proportion may have been closer to a tenth.[7] But a high proportion of slaves worked as domestic servants in substantial households, enjoying the certainty of three meals a day, a roof over their heads, and a good chance to build up a little savings and gain their liberty when they had passed middle age. Their children they might have to leave in their master's house to endure in turn some decades of servitude—a fair exchange, since many slaves came into their condition as the price for life itself, having been abandoned by their parents at birth and reared by their finders for later sale.[8] The exposing of children points to the very pinched circumstances of the free poor. Certainly they looked forward to a shorter adult life than the luckiest slaves of all, those that belonged to the emperor.[9] *Servi Caesaris* sometimes owned their own slaves, traveled in pomp and luxury on the emperor's business, commanded deference from all but the highest aristocracy, and after manumission vaulted to monied prominence among the freeborn. They did not typify life in servitude, of course, any more than those very different others who died in the mines of Dacia. But both extremes of fortune show the impossibility of lumping all slaves together.

It makes more sense to place at the bottom the free

poor. Their numbers we will never know, for there was no one to write it down, no one indeed from the literate classes to recognize poverty as a fit subject for polite conversation. Tombstones offer no help, either. None tells us that the deceased was penniless. Had that been so, he and his family could never have afforded the inscription. Archeology fails us, for no one has sought fame through the excavation of a slum. Only two aids are at hand: first, the many mentions of poverty appearing in the predictions of astrologers, which must surely have corresponded in some degree with common experience; second, analogies to be drawn with other periods better documented.[10] In fourteenth- and fifteenth-century Europe, as an illustration, one person in three lived in habitual want, that is, he devoted the vast bulk of each day's earnings to his immediate needs and accumulated no property or possessions to speak of. I would be surprised if the indigent of the Roman empire constituted much smaller a part of the total population. Their ranks were not fixed or frozen, to be sure; but as many left them by a premature death, dropping below the subsistence level,[11] as scrambled to safety above it, and as many joined their ranks by debt as managed to accumulate a little capital.[12] A dozen other signs scattered through the preceding pages—Rome's thousands on the dole, the cramped housing of an Egyptian town, the gleaners of a Judaean village—must all be added to the total of misery.

To sum up our survey (no part of which pretends to be very full or firm): we have at the top of Roman society a quite minute but extraordinarily prominent and rich nobility, itself split into a higher (senatorial) and a lower (equestrian) stratum; at the bottom, a large mass of the totally indigent, mostly free but partly slave; and strung out between the extremes a variety too heterogeneous to be called in any sense a middle class, counting in a small-town decurion as much as Cicero's beloved slave-secretary, Marcus Tullius Tiro. The chief purpose of the survey is to suggest what the proportions of the social scale must have felt like. "Verticality" is key to the understanding of it. Great were the differences between the extremes, attenuated the middle parts. The sense of high and low pressed heavily on the consciousness of both.

Whatever the setting, this stratification is pronounced. If we take the army as the mirror of society that it certainly was, we see toward the beginning of our period the division of spoils at Pompey's triumph: [13]

To his 20(?) staff officers	ca. 800,000 denarii each
To 50(?) legionary tribunes	ca. 180,000 denarii each
To 500(?) legionary centurions	ca. 30,000 denarii each
To 32,000 legionary privates	ca. 1,500 denarii each

A century later the imperial legion paid annually [14]

To 6 tribunes	unknown
To 1 centurion (*primus pilus*)	15,000 denarii
To 9 centurions (*primi ordinis*)	7,500 denarii
To 50 regular centurions	3,750 denarii
To 5,100 privates	225 denarii (up to 675 for advanced ranks)

And within stone-built legionary fortresses the allocation of space obeyed the same rules. The senator in command (*legatus*) sprawled amid his rich furnishings, decorated halls, and peristyle courtyard over an expanse of 75,000 square feet, while the trooper disposed his kit, bunk, and self in 50-odd square feet.[15] How small that made him feel!

Consider next the shape of property distribution in several villages in this period. Three of them are in Egypt (figure 1, light-colored bars), involving respectively eighty-nine Philadelphians in A.D. 217, 331 parcels of land at Crocodilopolis in 47, and sixty farmers of Karanis in 300–305. A fourth (figure 1, black bar) included sixty-seven lots for irrigation at Lamasba, fifty miles southwest of Cirta, in the early third century. For the Egyptian villages, areas are expressed in *arourai,* for Lamasba, the figures refer to *kapita* of unknown size, fifty-four people owning 70–799 *kapita;* six people, 800–1,999; another six, 1,200–3,900; and one person owning 4,000 *kapita.*[16] An assessment of 108 properties in two areas of Italy in the reign of Trajan reveals the same basic pattern (figure 2).[17]

I need not stress the less-than-scientific nature of the two graphs. Each of the half-dozen sets of figures that are used presents its own problems, among them, our uncertainty about the other properties that may have been owned elsewhere by persons on our lists. That of course would affect the pattern of wealth-distribution in an absolute sense, without, however, affecting ratios within the local setting. Despite difficulties of interpretation I think

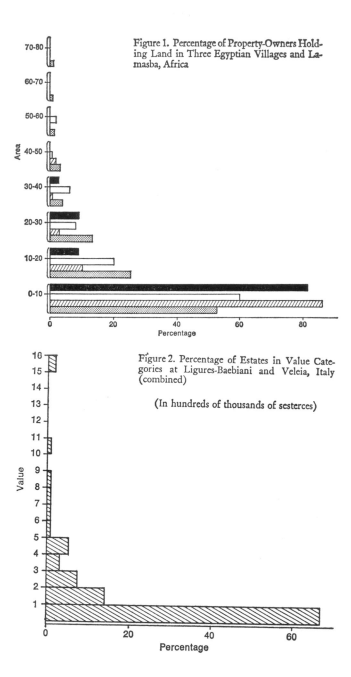

Figure 1. Percentage of Property-Owners Holding Land in Three Egyptian Villages and Lamasba, Africa

Figure 2. Percentage of Estates in Value Categories at Ligures-Baebiani and Veleia, Italy (combined)

(In hundreds of thousands of sesterces)

the graphs fairly express in visual terms what is salient in class proportions: verticality. Interlocking evidence abounds. We may recall from chapter 1 the small number of relatively rich people that villages contained; from the present chapter, the small number of officers in the army and the few decurions in cities. Perhaps that last proportion needs emphasis. It marked off the aristocracy from the masses in the most blatant fashion, so that, in the capital, Cicero can oppose to senators and *equites,* or to senators alone, "all citizens." In smaller centers, the two natural parts are "senate and people," and to observers of these scenes, the world consisted of only two classes, "the rich and the poor." [18]

The inward meaning of this opposition would be profoundly affected by one's chances of rising or falling on the social scale. Although on just this subject more has been written in the last two decades than in the preceding two centuries, the questions still outnumber the answers, particularly questions that concern the common man. Something has been said already about the flow of life between countryside and city, and we have encountered not only the ubiquitous traveling about of merchants but of artisans as well.[19] Was such movement likely to better them? We cannot be sure. Yet in the minds of contemporaries, traveling was an ill to be avoided,[20] as much so as the changing of the craft one was born into.

"A man is obliged to teach his son a trade, and whoever does not teach his son a trade teaches him to become a robber." That was the maxim of a rabbi.[21] In Egypt,

papyri allow a fairly close look at weaving, the most
widespread and economically the most important industry of the ancient world. It is common to find a pair
of brothers working at this together,[22] or some other indication of kin connections that might include slaves or
freedmen also. And the same tight texture of business
often appears in other provinces through their inscriptions: of husband and wife selling honey or purple dye,
of two brothers making pigments, of father and son turn-
ing out Arretine pottery or exporting oil or wine, or of a
dyer saluted as "the sixth of his line to head the shop."[23]
Very little of this kind of mention, however, provides
more than a glimpse at the range of possibilities. Welcome because it is concrete and vivid, it nevertheless
leaves unanswered the essential question, What was the
ratio of job changes as against inherited job stability?
Scholars can only be left to their general impression,
based on no proper documentation, that a man usually
took up whatever work his family handed down to him.

The same difficulty of interpretation meets us at a still
more crucial point. There is wide agreement that urban
conditions favored mobility far more than did rural. For
someone in manufacture and commerce on any scale at
all, the wheel of chance spun much faster than for the
man whose capital resided in land—hence, more rapid
changes in status. To borrow a medieval maxim, *Stadtluft
macht frei*. In Roman cities, however, while economic
vitality is obvious, we should remember how atomized industries were, how minutely subdivided into little shops

and little agencies.[24] Great fortunes rarely emerged among them. To be sure, once money accumulated, in whatever way, it was invested in all sorts of businesses by the wealthy—in tileries or potteries,[25] in bakeries or fulleries.[26] Commerce on a large scale enrolled or produced (we seldom can tell which) considerable capital that, most often in Italian maritime cities, we can pin down to specific cases and names.[27] Even on a small scale, "those who deal in goods and sell them, though they may be scourged by the aediles, must not be scorned as low persons. Indeed, it is not forbidden for people of this sort to seek the decurionate or some magistracy in their city; for they are not dishonored." [28] So likewise with petty professions. A poor man pondering a future for his son might think to himself, "I'll teach him a trade—a barber's or auctioneer's or indeed a lawyer's, for that's what the devil alone can take away from him." [29]

All this testimony earns a rather cautious acknowledgment that people who started with some minor skill or minor sum of money could indeed rise to relative affluence—could and did, in verifiable instances that aroused less surprise at their success than contempt of their origins. The already well-to-do invested their surplus in a wide range of not very large enterprises run for them by some other entrepreneur, free or freedman or slave, and drew from them a satisfactory return. From Italy at least, commerce reached out gainfully in all directions; it must be mere chance that evidence for big traders in other areas is so scanty.

A case in point is the third-century pretender, Firmus, said to be a merchant of Alexandria. His commerce involved great cargoes of glass, paper, and the other chief products of the eastern trade.[30] But a Roman who imported the same goods from Egypt to Puteoli earned only Cicero's scorn. Shiploads of paper, linen, and glass he thought were "empty things, for mere show";[31] and when a load of wheat came in from Alexandria to Athens with a value of some seventy thousand denarii a year, the dockside spectators talked it down with jokes about shipwrecks.[32] "What race of men would you call more wretched than traders and shippers?" asks the protagonist of a third-century historical novel. "They sail about seeking markets ill-supplied, dealing with local agents and petty retailers, borrowing at unholy rates and risking their heads."[33] "Whoever hopes he may grow rich by trade," runs a Roman epitaph, "will be fooled in his hopes."[34]

We cannot, perhaps, arrive at our goal: a reasonably close sense of the chances involved in various business careers. Still, I do not see signs of opportunities in commerce equal to the overwhelming proofs for both profits and investments in cash-crop farming (above, pp. 49–51). Agriculture attended by its characteristic social stability ruled the economy. It ruled even the lives and pursuits of cities. Alternative routes to riches and to the improvement of one's status were so jammed with the traffic of under-capitalized competitors and so beset with dangers and uncertainties that few traveled them very far.

Among those few, freedmen stood out. To that subject

we will return in a moment. We should note at this point, however, one peculiarity in the evidence that we must deal with. Since the freedman element was so large in Italy, and since Italy provides a majority of all known inscriptions, a majority of the literature useful for our study, and a majority of the litigation giving rise to our legal sources, it exerts a disproportionate influence on our impressions. It inclines us to believe in a degree of mobility empire-wide that really did not exist. In fact, even in the peninsula considerable continuity within the ruling class can be shown.[35] It becomes far more the rule than the exception as one moves eastward. Specific studies of individual cities supply no better proof than the recurrent phrase, "like his ancestors," which decorates complimentary references to so many local citizens: "applauded like his ancestors for his manner of life and the honor in which he is held," "of the magistrates' class from his ancestors," and so on.[36] The monopolizing of leadership by a narrow circle, generation after generation, is cause for no surprise. Given the high cost of office-holding and the unimpressive totals of community wealth that Parium and Tymandus illustrate, we should expect nothing else.

In an economy that was by our standards stagnant, large fortunes seem to have been made not so much by individual enterprise as by mere chance. A satirist explains how, in an imaginary conversation between the god of commerce and the god of wealth. Says Hermes, "I know plenty of men suddenly rich," to which Ploutos replies, "It's death that does it" [37]—meaning inheritances. Granted, the scene is fiction; but, drawing on hundreds of true happenings, astrologers of the second, third, and fourth centuries responded to their clients in terms of the same probabilities.[38] Trade there was, and one had one's craft to practice. There were business opportunities and rewards for hard work, good luck, and the use of one's wits. But when told that one would soon be rich, one could only look to a legacy or a marriage for the source. Legacy- and heiress-hunting attracted most attention among the upper classes. It was a game played there for higher stakes, drawing more familiar, more caustic comments from both Greek and Latin satirists. But at every level it infected relations between the Haves and the Have-nots with an extra element of falseness and servility. As another fragment of imaginary conversation runs,

> In this town it's not the pursuit of one's studies that is talked about, eloquence has no standing, frugality and high morals don't produce the reward of praise. No, any man you may see in this town, let me tell you, belongs to one of two classes, the legacy-hunters or the hunted. In this town nobody raises children. Whoever has his own heirs won't be asked to dinner parties or the theater. He's locked out of the nice things, just stuck off in a corner among the no-accounts. But if he never married and has no near relatives, he gets the top rank.[39]

Trimalchio is typical.[40] He gave himself body and soul to his master, suppressed all pride. A fortune fell to him exactly as he hoped, and he somersaulted into a grand house and fame. The manners he assumed with his master he found perfectly natural among his guests: falseness and servility.

He is typical also in being an ex-slave, belonging thus to the truly liberated. No family honor, no inherited code, no national or caste customs restrain him from the free exploitation of every means to the one end, money. He and his like in the history of the empire constitute to an extraordinary degree the element of vigor, thrust, and venture. They learned from their master what counted—wealth—and as their master's surrogates in occupations beneath contempt, they learned how to run a shop that he financed, how to practice a trade to which he apprenticed them, and how to handle his accounts before they themselves had any accounts to keep. In their dealings with him they learned how to please, how to hide what they really felt, and how to deceive. "Let the buyer beware!" And when he turned adrift those who did not please him, they learned from his harshness, too. In Rome, a third to a half of the population in the early Empire that showed on their tombstones no office, no trade, in short, nothing but a bare name, were slaves, ex-slaves, and people of recent slave origin; in Pompeii, the same proportion belonged to the governing aristocracy.[41] The two figures suggest how intense must have been the struggle simply to stay alive in freedom and how large must have been the number of competitors. Only the fittest survived. The figures suggest also the difference between the competition at Rome, against a population of a half-million or more, and at Pompeii, among twenty thousand. Far to the north and south of Pompeii, in sleepier provincial towns and countryside, freedmen found still greater scope for their unprincipled energies.[42]

Their descendants constituted a major element among the decurions of Pannonia and Africa. Nouveaux riches of this sort with their sudden successes deeply shocked the master class. Juvenal in his satires spoke for a wide prejudice. Petronius reflected a general aristocratic disgust at Trimalchio's whole story, especially at the vulgarity that marked everything Trimalchio did and said. In reaction, the master class first defined and then punished freedmen.

They defined them by law, making of them a separate group that owed continued reverence, duties, and payments to the men whom they had once served. Failure to render specified services could be litigated; failure to render homage, a more elusive due, brought on a passionate debate in the Roman senate. "Things have come to such a pass that ex-slaves treat with their former masters on a footing of 'rights' and equality, spurn their opinions, threaten a blow of the fist unprovoked, and make a joke of punishment with impunity." What had happened to the relationship of condescending assistance on the one hand, grateful deference on the other? As a devout abolitionist put it a century ago, she "was glad to see the Negroes losing some of their old servility but sorry that they were no longer very obedient." [43]

The senate's debate thus went on to consider the possibility of making ex-slaves wear some special uniform. In that way their derelictions could not escape notice. Though the idea came to nothing, the taint of a servile origin could generally be sniffed out in a man's name. The changing of Lucius Crassicius Pasicles, let us say, to

Pansa (a Greek cognomen to a good Roman one) became illegal by decree of the emperor Claudius.[44] Of course, civic status could be checked in the municipal registry, too. Freedmen, however, were more easily and invidiously picked out on public occasions when their whole rank might be excluded as a block or offered a segregated and lesser share in a banquet or largesse.[45] At private dinners they got the least honored seat—naturally, for they were equally debarred from all the various routes by which they might have won respect. They could not serve in the legions, they could not aim at municipal magistracies.[46] Those who formed any sexual connection with a free woman of a higher class, senatorial or equestrian, risked capital punishment. If (having the wealth to qualify) a freedman advertised himself as an *eques,* he could be arraigned in court.[47]

Passion in debate and harshness in law met the ambitious freedman not, of course, in the company of ordinary folk [48] but higher on the social scale, where those above him struggled to preserve their precious prerogatives. They shuddered at the demeaning of the consulship by unworthy holders; [49] indignantly they watched an ex-slave, however rich, claiming precedence over Romans of good family, or having the impudence to offer gentlemen advice and assistance, just as if he were freeborn.[50] Such conduct broached the boundaries of class, and class, whatever term the Greeks and Romans used for it, it was the duty of every citizen to preserve not only by his own fitting behavior but by a prompt rebuke to anyone that tried to rise too high. "Rank must be preserved," said Cicero.

Four centuries later, Libanius in Antioch was still repeating, "Whatever one's rank, it must be maintained." [51]

Stratification was minute. The tiny senatorial order contained patricians, consulars, praetorians, and ordinary members. Their wives and daughters enjoyed an equally particularized honor.[52] Next, equestrians, among whom those who served the emperor "with a state mount" (*equo publico,* as the phrase went) stood out. It was a Roman invention to set aside certain adjectives for certain dignities: "Most Grand" for ex-consuls, "Most Renowned" for ordinary senators, "Most Distinguished" or "Distinguished" for *equites* of all sorts from Cicero's day on, and in townships, "Most Splendid" or "Splendid," while "Illustrious" described the upper equestrian rungs as a whole.[53] "Most Eminent," "Most Perfect," and "Outstanding" designated what we would call civil service grades. We have nothing to show whether such adjectives were used in ordinary introductions or spoken address, but they certainly figured in formal documents.

Corresponding to the last three titles, one might also call oneself *vir sexagenarius, centenarius, ducenarius,* or *trecenarius,* showing in sesterces what one was paid as a "Sixty-," "One-," "Two-," or "Three-hundred-Thousand Man," just as if a civil servant today were to list himself in the telephone book as "Jones ($20,000)." Behind the titles lay the same pride that advertised to the penny the size of philanthropic gifts, or governed one's general dress and conduct in public. Wealth declared itself as one of many signs of rank. A senator's wife could be spotted from a distance in the streets of Rome. Her luxurious litter marked her, as well as the elaboration of her jewels, dress, and hair,[54] while her husband stood out more plainly still because of the broad crimson stripe on his toga and the lunette sewn to his shoes.[55] Such a person went about with a grand and showy retinue.[56] His motive hardly needs nexplanation: he sought status. "So many slaves attended him, so many freedmen and clients, that whatever word he spoke was the talk of the town." [57]

However much senators and equestrians valued the town's opinion, they competed more keenly still for the respect of their peers. In that competition, affluence obviously constituted one important factor. It is a factor next to impossible to disentangle from many others. Trimalchio's failure to win respectability, at least in the eyes of his creator, raises our first question, whether money by itself was enough. Clearly it was not, among the very uppermost strata. They laughed at ill-educated slips and slurs of speech;[58] the old school tie, as we would say, was flourished in eastern cities by the class of "gymnasium graduates." [59] Those who went on to advanced training in rhetoric and a career of eloquence were hailed by crowds of supporters and laudatory decrees, by claques and plaques. Here then is a second factor: great learning, great power as a speaker, style and taste in one's address. But among persons celebrated for all these attributes, a surprising majority represented the second, third, or fourth generation of talent and wealth combined.[60] Hence yet another consideration: the inheritance of one's place. It meets us, for example, in the pairing of words used to define distinction, "by family and wealth." [61] Pedigree would be a matter of common knowledge, announced in one's very name. While "Weaver" or "Carpenter" declared plebeian origins, while "Rogatus" or "Rogatianus" (formed from a past participle) was likely to show provincial, African, origin, and a Greek name encountered in Rome would point to servile descent,[62] in contrast "Licinius" brought instantly to mind the most admired connections. A name was a precious possession, identical with one's clan, indeed synonymous with "family." The theft of it by an outsider was punishable at law.[63]

To pay for the enormously expensive role in the community that would, over the span of some generations, ennoble one's line; to pay the fees and voluntary subscriptions to the gymnasium through which one's culture and accent might satisfy polite circles; to maintain one's household in proper fashion—all required a handsome income. It was taken for granted by the aristocracy. Without it, social ambitions could never be treated seriously. By itself, however, it did not constitute respectability. On the other hand, when we turn from what was expected of a Roman senator to a decurion of Tymandus (some of whose peers could barely read or write), we confront quite another scale of values. The army veteran, even more explicitly, points the difference. It was not his years in camp that brought him honor, it was not likely to be his lineage, and hardly his cultivation. His neighbors valued him because, as one says, "He's *got* it"—meaning money alone.[64] His mustering-out bonus and his savings allowed an ex-private to assume the leadership of a village, an officer to enter the council of some large provincial center. Both were of course supposed to assert their claims in tangible form. If they did that, not simply through having money but through spending it in the usual sequence of municipal offices, priesthoods, and benefactions, nothing more was asked of them.

To rise in the world, one must be a man of means. That much is clear, as is the difficulty of acquiring means through pursuits we would asume today: industry and commerce. To rise to real heights required much else besides—not least, time. Honor must mature and ancestors accumulate. One's upward steps would be noted in the community, in frequent well-attended gatherings that brought people together in public to size each other up not only according to the obvious distinction of magistrates from masses, proedria from indiscriminate seating, but according to repute and display. What anthropologists would call a "shame society" was of course a "pride society" too. The upper classes emphasized, for everyone to notice and acknowledge, the steep, steep social structure that they topped.

The broader distinction between plebeian and everything else above it was fiercely defended—needless to say, by the upper class. Passage upward by the most natural routes, first through enrolled citizenship in a municipality, then through election to the higher magistracies, began gradually to be blocked by custom, and custom received reinforcement from law.[65] "The rich" and "the poor," "the great" and "the little" thus appear under new names, "the More Honorable" and "the More Lowly." A recent book by Peter Garnsey describes how the latter could not bring suit against their superiors, were obliged to put up security when they assumed the guardianship of a minor, and, if they committed a crime, suffered much crueler punishments.[66] Discrimination, at least in Italy, bestowed on them an assignment to the least respected voting tribes and a smaller portion of cash, food, wine, or whatever else might be distributed on public occasions.[67] The underlying principle was a familiar one: "To him who hath shall be given."

Secure in interlaced wealth, acquaintance, and kinship, gentlemen earned yet another nickname: "the Haughty." They earned it by conspicuous consumption expressive of their vast resources and, by implication, an insult to the poor. They earned it by their progress through the streets, sweeping *hoi polloi* to the walls. And they earned it by just the same gestures and expressions of face we use today to show hauteur—torso tilted back, nose in the air, eyebrows raised.[68] " 'I am superior to you,' " Epictetus imagines one of them saying, " 'for my father has consular rank.' Another says, 'I have been a tribune and you have not.' And if we were horses, you would be saying, 'My sire was swifter than yours,' or 'I have quantities of barley and fodder.' " A boast of influence was equally common, equally absurd. "If you tell me, 'I can deliver a mighty kick,' I shall say to you in my turn, 'You take pride in the act of a donkey.' "[69] And in a longer passage Epictetus goes on to describe the price paid for rank.

> You will have to borrow some paltry slaves, and possess a few pieces of silver plate, and exhibit these same pieces conspicuously and frequently, if you can, and try not to let people know that they are the same, and possess con-

temptible bright clothes, and all other kinds of finery,
and show yourself off as the one who is honored by the
most distinguished persons, and try to dine with them, or
at least make people think that you dine with them; and
resort to base arts in the treatment of your person, so as
to appear more shapely and of gentler birth than you actually are. All these contrivances you must adopt.[70]

Nothing rewarded such efforts more richly than the
power they afforded to insult someone else in a lower
station. Invite him to dinner and he came, sure to be
shown a place at table that demeaned him, a serving of
food that left him hungry, cheap wine, and the insolence
of the servants—servants in this respect taught by their
master. The insults he handed out had to be swallowed
along with the dinner, so long as his guests had nothing
better waiting for them at home.[71] "Unhappy poverty has
nothing about it harder to bear than that it makes men the
target of ridicule"—so said Juvenal, and others echoed
him.[72]

The mockery and scorn they endured was deliberate,
unprovoked, and unresisted. In the very streets it pursued
them. But it was better to be rudely ignored by "the
Haughty" than to be stopped, bullied, and humiliated by
some young drunken blueblood.[73] By a somersault of luck,
it might even be a nobleman who saved one. A stranger
coming late into town in Palestine was picked up by the
nightwatchmen, who would have given him a good beating and a night in jail for no reason at all, had he not
said he was known to the household of one of the city
magnates.[74]

A special shame attached to people who made a public spectacle of themselves. That was what hurt so much about Nero's craze for Greek shows: young men of good family had to put themselves on display in the theater like common actors. Bankrupts the whole city would know and might pillory in its own way, by a sort of inversion of proedria. They might be made to sit in a part of the theater set aside for them.[75] A public beating disqualified one from the decurionate, likewise the job of collecting sales taxes in the marketplace, because that involved continual wrangling with petty hucksters. Auctioneers might be disqualified because they made a living out of a loud voice in crowded places. Only "the More Lowly" could risk such occupations. "Those whose lives lie in unnoticed strata, if they do anything amiss . . . , few know of it. Their obscurity and their poverty are a match for each other."

Whether it was the community as a whole that passed judgment or whether it was no more than a company of a dozen at dinner before whom one's insignificance was held up to ridicule, clearly the sense of hierarchy ruled behavior. Its various steps were explicitly marked off by an uncontested right to assert one's superiority in offensive, often cruel, ways. The key word *publicness* of the preceding chapter combines with the *verticality* emphasized in this present one to explain, or go far toward explaining, the explicit assertion of status, defended with increasing arrogance and harshness by all kinds of legal distinctions.

Since it was "the powerful" who made the law, the same men felt free to subordinate the law to the higher claims of peer loyalty, patronage, and favoritism. Details of the ways in which these considerations came into play are clearly detectible through a screen of euphemisms showing what was expected of the parties involved: from petitioners for help, deference to those who might help them; from peers exchanging letters on the preferment of a younger man or on the handling of a case to be litigated, the most delicate phraseology. Pliny writes in illustration, "Many people, in their wish not to seem to be a party too much to the influence of the powerful, gain a reputation for maladresse or even spitefulness." One could, he says, be fair to all conditions, one could reward merit; but a gentleman would not.[76]

Beyond deference, the powerful also exacted bribes, on a small scale but as a matter of habit. Their petty venality was known to everybody. In the army, soldiers had to bribe their officers. "I hope to live frugally," writes a new recruit to his father, "but nothing gets done here without money, and testimonials don't help at all unless one helps oneself." [77] The same discovery was to be made in dealing with officials of the central government, from the emperor's slaves (how else but by taking bribes did they grow so rich?) up to the really great predators like Pallas and Narcissus under Nero.[78] And the equestrian had to get his due, too. "Send him a bushel of olives and some fish, since we want to make use of him"; "Buy some presents for the Isis festival for the persons we usually send them to, especially the district supervisors"; "Help us poor peasants, who gain our daily bread by the labor of our hands, for we are outmatched by the chief estate-lessee and the great favor he has won with the procurator through his lavish presents"; "I sent you through Ammonius a dish of quails, two jars of black fish sauce, and a dish of sweet cakes." [79] Pitiful offerings! Tribute from the helpless offered up to the vanity of the powerful, lessons in corruption taught to the less fastidious pride and to the more realistic avarice of the servants of "the More Honorable." These little sweeteners accompanying the address of a poor man to a great were made still more welcome by abject deference. "The humble man humiliates himself in a disgraceful and undignified manner, throwing himself headlong to the ground upon his knees, clothing himself in a beggar's rags, and heaping dust upon himself." [80] It was a posture that invited verbal kicks delivered indiscriminately to the whole body of the *vulgus* by Horace, Martial, Juvenal, Seneca, Tacitus (especially Tacitus), and other Latin authors.[81] A better defined contempt struck specific targets by name: weavers, fullers, and so on.[82] Cicero, speaking, as it happens, about the eastern regions, sweeps into the waste bin half their population of "craftsmen, petty shopkeepers, and all that filth of the cities." [83]

A sort of rationale underlay, or more likely overlay, his disgust—for we can only guess whether a reason begot a prejudice or the other way around. In any case, he shared with others a view that hand-labor coarsened body, soul, and manners.[84] Since the better part of man was mental and spiritual, whoever depended on mere physical powers for his living lived that much lower. Beyond such philosophizing, soldering or dyeing or digging were all dirty,

ugly work. No person of refined taste could bear to be a
smith, a tanner, a butcher,[85] neither could the freeborn
bear to acknowledge someone else as master. "The very
wages of a laborer," says Cicero, "are the badges of
slavery." [86]

Because a higher civilization came to the Romans in
the guise of slaves, suppliants, and captives, they regarded
many Greek arts as beneath them. It was astonishing to
Valerius Maximus that a Roman, "although a citizen of
the highest nobility . . . , devoted his genius to a sordid
pursuit"—painting. "I am not led to include painters
within the liberal arts, no more than sculptors or workers
in marble or the servants of luxury," Seneca concurred.
"Roman seriousness does not yet cultivate [the medical
science] of the Greeks, so very few of our citizens touch
such a great source of profit"—that from the elder Pliny.
And back to Cicero: "Public opinion divides the trades
and professions into the liberal and the vulgar. . . . The
work of the artisan is degrading. There is nothing noble
about a workshop . . . but [medicine] or architecture and
teaching at the advanced level, from which society derives
the greatest benefit, are considered honorable occupations
for those to whose social position they are appropriate." [87]

So much for the various "craftsmen" that Cicero dis-
missed; but what was wrong with "petty tradesmen"?
The answer to that question lay in their dependence on
falsehood. It was their business to lie about their wares, a
thing that no honorable man was capable of doing.[88] The
same charge could be made against a slave, that his position required deception. "No one of a servile background

can develop any great pride." "It belongs to slavery not to speak for or against anyone you wish." "When you see someone cringing before another or fawning on him against his real opinion, you can with confidence say this fellow is no free man." [89] And against the poor, too, the charge could be made that their very poverty reduced them to lying, cheating, stealing. The rich frankly confessed that only themselves could afford to be honest.[90] A handsome admission! —leading into a half-glimpsed line of argument that the same men taught their slaves to flatter and lie, their freedmen to exult in liberated impudence, the huckster to cry up his worst wares as his best, and the hungry to steal and kill, so that everything vicious in the plebeian world could be said to spring from the vices of the More Honorable. Though the steps in such reasoning appear as isolated parts of various passages in various authors, we could hardly expect them to be followed out in suicidal sequence by any large number of the nobility.

Instead, a final, circular argument was much more commonly invoked: The poor deserve to be held in contempt because they have no money. Poverty in and of itself is "vile," "dishonored," "ugly," [91] for the same reason that "petty trade is sordid, but if it is large and extensive, importing many goods from all over and offering them for sale without deception, it is not too shameful; rather, if in satiety or, better, in contentment it retreats from the harbor to country estates, it seems most rightfully deserving of praise." [92] The speaker is our friend Cicero again, the self-made man whose exquisite adaptability to the

values around him make him the best reporter we could
ask for. We may take it as a true reflection of late Republican upper-class Roman morality, then, that in his mind
the two words "rich" and "honorable" belong together
and thus appear so regularly in his speeches arm in arm,
like a happily married couple.[93] When he and his like in
that period turned to the ruling of an empire, they naturally imposed their views on the whole structure of society.
From "the good and rich" they chose witnesses and guar-
dians, candidates for admission to the innermost parts of
their state, decurions to run the towns and judges to sit
on the bench.[94] True, it could be argued that these
positions involved heavy expenses; that (as we have seen)
a person already rich could be more often counted on to
rise above the crimes and vices that were forced on poverty; in short, that logically defensible reasons supported
the placing of the wealthy in all positions of trust and
power. But when we get right down to it, wealth seems to
earn respect by itself, to the degree it is accumulated.

A spectrum of approbation was applied by Cicero as by
other writers. At one end lay the very best thing of all,
wealth without a person's having to get it himself, that
is, inherited. The active pursuit of it aroused certain
misgivings,[95] at least among the topmost nobility. They
simply *had* money. Next along the spectrum lay wealth
enjoyed in retirement; and verging toward the unrespect-
able, wealth still in the process of accumulation. We can
discover another spectrum, too. Romans are actually
found declaring, "After all, money isn't everything." This
is a confession that a cynic would expect to hear from

very rich men—Sallust, Cicero, Seneca—long after they
had built up their fortunes, and not always by means that
would bear inspection.[96] At the other extreme lay the
exuberant greed spelled out prominently in a Pompeian
mosaic, "Long live profits!"[97] and the bitter honesty of
the saying, "Good is the smell of profits, from whatever
derived."[98] The Romans indeed acknowledged a goddess
called Money (*Pecunia*); but some of them were blinder
devotees than others, and her cult was tributary to another,
Status (*Philotimia*).[99]

Status got in the way of charity, once more by a circular
argument. While the empire had its share of kindly men
and women who felt real distress at someone else's suffering and tried to lighten it by their generosity, all this was
on an individual basis. Once the problem of suffering was
looked at *en masse,* different feelings took over. Broadcast
distributions to the whole populace were, as we have seen,
very frequent features of city life or, for that matter, of
life in various subdivisions like crafts associations and
urban wards; but cash or food was handed out by rank,
more for the upper classes, the decurions, officers, or whatever, than for the ordinary citizens or members.[100] Honor
qualified, rarely need. As to need, the More Honorable
threw up their hands. "Most people think the problem of
poverty is insoluble." "To certain people I shall not give,
even though there is need, because there will still be need
even if I give." And beyond these baffled or uncaring senti-
ments, note a semantic clue: the words that Greeks and
Romans used for "idle" leaned more toward "lazy" than
(through no fault of one's own) "unemployed." That

explains a Pompeian's declaration, written up on a wall, "I hate poor people. If anyone wants something for nothing, he's a fool. Let him pay up and he'll get it." [101]

Poor people returned the hatred. A number of passages testify to this, at any rate as it was sensed by the rich.[102] Little came of it since, in the last resort, the urban like the rural lower classes had little power to assert their resentment. Instead, they accepted their lot without thinking much about it, indeed, very much on its own terms with its own ups and downs. So much we may infer from their passivity, silence, and deference. They did not see around them signs of enough change or chance to question their condition. There could be no revolution of rising expectations when in fact few expected to rise.

"Rise" is of course relative anyway, not only by comparison of the end with the starting point but in terms also of the whole distance that may in theory be traversed. Who among us seriously aspires to be, like a Roman senator, among the richest and most powerful two ten-thousandths of one percent within his own society? Who gives it a second thought? Like ourselves, the Roman in his one-room shop, in the back of which he and his wife and children slept and in the front of which he spent the day making and selling (let us say) articles of felt, did not look forward to a future altogether without prospects. He could realistically aim at an apprenticeship for his son and the lad's help in the business later. He could realistically aim at the secretaryship of his craft's local guild. While he might buy from an astrologer the promise of an inheritance, just as today he buys a state lottery ticket,

when he turned from fantasy to fact he found much to
give significance and self-respect to his life. It was only
from the standpoint of a gentleman of high education,
owner of a couple of slaves—such a man as Juvenal—that
the petty craftsman or tradesman seemed to have no
future. Modern historians of the Empire who look at Juvenal's
world only through his eyes (or Cicero's, or Tacitus') still
speak of "the vital minimum for a Roman to exist on"
as no less than 5,000 denarii in unearned annual income.
Below that, sheer beggary! —though it needs no pointing
out how great a majority would in fact have been well
content with a tenth of that sum.[103] Modern historians
speak also of "the contempt the ancient felt for any servile
activity . . . ; all paid work was held in contempt." [104]
Had it really been so, Trimalchio would never have com-
missioned for his own house a wall-painting that showed
him being bought and sold as a slave, nor would an auctioneer, a shopkeeper, a weaver, a fuller, or any member
of the "despised" occupations have advertised on his tombstone for all to see, down through eternity, exactly what
work he did and where in the city he did it. Only the
More Honorable despised him, too many miles above his
head to matter. "Great is work," proclaimed a teacher in
Palestine, "for every craftsman walks out with the imple-
ments of his calling, and is proud of them. Thus the
weaver walks out with a shuttle behind his ear. The dyer
walks out with wool behind his ear. The scribe walks out
with his pen behind his ear. All are proud of their
craft." [105]

V

WHAT FOLLOWS

On the threshold of our period and on the threshold of a civil war, a famous moment presents itself to historians. Caesar stirs his horse to a trot and splashes across the river Rubicon. It marks the boundaries of his province. To cross it in arms is treason. As he considers his decision, he passes in mental review a variety of social blocs and classes, each one with its own sympathies and antipathies: the resentment of the unenfranchised in the north of the peninsula, the loyalty of his legions, the ambitions of the business interests and small-town aristocracy. From among all these forces, if he leads, what follows? It is the following as much as his leading that makes the moment.

He must know and reflect on the train of relationships that transmits his will to the masses, from men of relatively or extremely educated, rich, and honored background in his immediate retinue to the peasant lad who must be induced to sign up under the banners of revolution—or at least induced *not* to join Pompey and the senate. He must sense the reality behind a whole dictionary of special terms—clientage, *vicinitas, ordo, gens* and *patria potestas, amicitia, fides, gratia*—in which contemporaries conceived what we would call Roman social relations. It is the study of the synapses that shows how waves of energy traveled through the body politic and made it move to war or peace. Without such study we know only Caesar and his horse.

Within the inner circle of Caesar's staff and friends or of their equivalent at other periods in Roman history, the historian looks around quite at his ease, confident that he understands pretty well what made people tick. He understands, that is, the senate and the equestrian class. Social relations connecting them with the remaining 99 percent of the population are, however, little known and little investigated. Moreover, as the preceding chapters will have shown, it is easier—there is more evidence—to show the negative side of those relations than the positive. For a variety of reasons, strata appear as exclusive. The senator of less means but older family wants to assert the importance of lineage against a newer member of the order; both unite against another from Asia. Hence, three standards of prestige: time, money, place. The farther back . . . , the more . . . , the closer to Rome . . .—these were the lines of thought drawn defensively around one's position to keep others out. A fourth we may call vaguely, culture. One might fail by the test of the first three and yet sneer at one's patron, as Lucian did at his employers [1] or as the dinner guests sneered at Trimalchio. Trimalchio, to be sure, paid a left-handed homage to the cultivation he lacked, but wisely took his stand on money. His creator, Petronius, in a royal court that honored Greeks, freedmen, and such less refined refinements of life as ten-course banquets and pretty slave boys, retreated into fastidiousness. He collected china.

Those were of course only the nice distinctions among the already distinguished. Broader differences marked off urban from rural, free from slave, upper class from lower. Broad or narrow, differences present themselves to our view as forces of repulsion. How then could they be bridged? That is, how could Caesar's will reach down to recruit a peasant? And why did the peasant or the urban poor, together a vast majority in the whole empire, not rise in revolt, seize all wealth, and rule it for themselves?

Fear of force, failure, and retaliation are obvious parts of an answer. Deference and division enter in as well. As to deference, the steep slope of society drew the eye upward. Rank was so clear, the sense of high and low so present to the consciousness, and its degrees made known so conspicuously in manners, dress, accent, cult, style, and material possessions, that it suppressed challenge. People at all levels knew their place.[2] They had in fact little chance to learn any other. An economy by our standards stagnant taught supplication, not energetic enterprise. When the astrologer held out great expectations, it was not in terms of a business success or a corner on the grain supply. His customers would never have swallowed *that*. Instead he promised them inheritance or a rich marriage. For most people (not for all; the picture is not entirely a still-life) change in fortune came mysteriously from above. All they could do was wait for it cap in hand, humble themselves to "the powerful," and be patient.

As to division, smoothed over in this essay through my aiming at general truths, it not only distinguished one time from another but one community or region from another. For example, freedmen enjoyed greater chances to rise in the world than the freeborn poor, and freedmen made up a much larger part of the population in Italy than, say, in Syria. Trade- and crafts-associations were much more common in Italy than in Syria, too; and the display of the most vulgar, aggressive arrogance was more a Roman than a Greek trait. So were individual big farms as opposed to villages, and the ignoring of vestigial democratic features in Italian towns as opposed to those in the eastern provinces. The hyphen in "Greco-Roman" civilization stands by abbreviation for many significant differences, within which still others set at odds "the dull Boeotians," "deceitful Carthaginians," "volatile Alexandrians," and so forth, each caricatured by jealous neighbors.[3] Finally, as we have seen, villages, urban voting tribes, and age-group associations occasionally clashed in quarrels expressive of fierce, narrow loyalties.

The concentration of wealth by the local aristocracy was thus not challenged by the *united* Have-nots. Their social impulse instead drew them into the more comfortable embrace of units of a few hundreds, in which they could find at least some of the pleasures denied them by the city as a whole. They appealed to the Haves to play patron, just as the community did on a larger scale and as a single client might on a smaller scale. Whether the division involved large or small groups, its relations with its patron were thus based on deference. He in turn was granted the right to command. Ultimately, that right rested on wealth. Modern historians may be right in thinking that what made the sharp inequities in the ancient economy bearable and kept social tensions within control was the willingness of the rich to supply to their fellow citizens the good things in life unconstrained. In early times that meant national security. The rich commanded because they alone could afford the most effective military equipment. In the Empire, it meant the amenities of a higher civilization: public banquets, theatrical presentations, temples, and the rest. An electoral slogan painted upon a Pompeian wall tells the whole story: "The united street-neighbors urge the election of So-and-So for magistrate. He will provide a four-pair gladiatorial show." What motive in turn inspired the candidate? Simply the love of status, *Philotimia*. No word, understood to its depths, goes farther to explain the Greco-Roman achievement. So far as I know, it has yet to receive the compliment of a scholarly treatise.

Wealth, being most safely lodged in land, changed hands slowly, in fact, ever more slowly. Over the centuries of our period, it became increasingly concentrated in fewer, bigger holdings. That phenomenon likewise still awaits a study. The primacy of land as an investment had several important consequences. It governed the relation, generally one of absentee-ownership, between country and city, peasant and decurion. I have described that in the first two chapters. Moreover, it diminished social mobility; for where wealth held the key to advancement, the more slowly it changed hands, the more slowly people changed status. Class hardened almost to the point of caste, at least in the late Empire. Finally, it gave other kinds of investment a bad name. Industry and commerce were not for gentlemen.

Each of these consequences may be followed out in long and instructive lines of interpretation. To take only the third and last, in the sketchiest fashion: What could have induced the Romans to be so blind? Surely they saw that, in their gathering of wealth by conquest, they gathered a giant market. Surely *someone* realized that the great swelling of cities in later Republican Italy offered perfectly extraordinary economic opportunities, especially in luxury goods, services, trades, and crafts. But no; with unteachable conservatism, rich Romans turned to the land, and even those of relatively modest means could not lower themselves to the running of an arms factory or fuller's mill. That left a vacuum, promptly filled by Greek freedmen. Their success in its upper levels (though we must not forget the vastly greater numbers of failures) was phenomenal, not only in Pompeii, but, by emigration, in a host of towns in Africa Proconsularis or Pannonia. The manners and values manifested by the likes of Trimalchio, prominent as provincial decurions, had the profoundest effect on the civilization of the empire.

We know about Trimalchio because one member of the literate classes considered him worthy of really complete excoriation. Only contempt roused his creator to the effort. Other members of the aristocracy indeed consider such subjects of social history—rarely, and with apology. Dio Chrysostom attempts an essay on poverty and prejudice. He abjures the polling of the poor. That would take too much time. Whatever needs to be known can be learned easily enough, he says, from the poets Homer, Hesiod, and Sophocles; and he must be excused for going into the subject at any length at all. Ammianus Marcellinus anticipates in his readers a similar impatience: "Not everything deserves narration that goes on among the lower orders." In contrast, Marc Bloch: "I can hardly be persuaded that it is perfectly legitimate to describe a state, without first having tried to analyze the society on which it rests." [4] Two views, ancient and modern. Which shall we follow?

ABBREVIATIONS

In the Appendixes and Notes, I use the usual abbreviations of sources and periodicals (they can be seen in *L'Année philologique,* for example), and the usual ones also for papyri (see M. David and B. A. van Groningen, *Papyrological Primer,* ed. 4, 1965, pp. 6–13), but in addition a few that may be less familiar:

Bab.	*Babylonian Talmud,* ed. I. Epstein, 1935–52
ESAR	*An Economic Survey of Ancient Rome,* ed. T. Frank, 1933–40
*FIRA*²	*Fontes iuris Romani antejustiniani,* ed. S. Riccobono, J. Baviera et al., 1940–43
*SEHRE*²	M. Rostovtzeff, *Social and Economic History of the Roman Empire* ², ed. P. M. Fraser, 1957

APPENDIX A

SUBDIVISIONS OF THE CITY

1. ADMINISTRATIVE

Rome was divided by Augustus into 14 *regiones* and 265 *vici* (Suet., *Aug.* 30.1; Plin., *N. H.* 3.66; the chief epigraphic evidence in *CIL* 6.975); the number of *vici* later rose above 300 (F. Castagnoli, *Topografia e urbanistica di Roma antica* [1969] 47 f.). They existed in the Republic in a semi-official form, since we hear of the organizing of crowds *vicatim* (Cic., *Pro Sestio* 34; *De domo sua* 54 and 129), the conducting of a census by Caesar *vicatim, per dominos insularum* (Suet., *Iul.* 41.3), and the supervising of *compitalia* from early times by *magistri vicorum*. See Castagnoli 47 and S. Panciera, *Archeologia classica* 22 (1970) 162. The cross-roads cult dated to Servius Tullius (Dionys. 4.14) and had its festival with *ludi* in December or January.

Certain Roman *vici* bore the name of a trade at some time dominant in them:

vicus [. . .]*ionum ferrariarum* (*CIL* 6.9185)

vicus turarius (Porph. on Hor., *Ep.* 1.20.1, ed. F. Hauthal, vol. I p. 505)

vicus vitrarius (*Libellus de reg. urbi Romae*, ed. A. Nordh [1949] p. 73)

vicus unguentarius (ibid. 85)

vicus sandaliarius, with the shrine of the Apollo so-named there (Suet., *Aug.* 57; Aul. Gell. 18.4.1)

vicus cornicularius (L. Moretti, *Archeologia class.* 10 [1958] 231–234)

vicus lorarius (*CIL* 6.9796)

vicus pulverarius (*CIL* 6.975)

vicus materiariorum (*CIL* 6.975)

Vici also occur elsewhere in Italy in a dozen cities, see *ILS* vol. III p. 673, including

Pisaurum (*CIL* 11.6367, *magistri vici* mentioned)

Ariminum (*CIL* 11.377, 379, and 417, seven *vici*, some with Roman names)

Volcei (*CIL* 10.415)

Spoletum (*CIL* 11.4815, *magistri vicorum* mentioned)

Ostia (*ILS* 5395, *magistri vici;* further, R. Meiggs, *Roman Ostia* [1960] 222)

Puteoli (*EE* 8.365, *clivus vitriarius sive vicus turarius* and *ILS* 6322, *inquilini vici;* further, *RE* s.v. Puteoli [M. Frederiksen, 1959] 2057; C. Dubois, *Pouzzoles antique* [1907] 238 f.)

Pompeii (*CIL* 4.60, pre-46 B.C.; further, M. Della Corte, *Case ed abitanti di Pompeii*² [1954] 255 and 286, four *vicomagistri* per *vicus*)

Turris Libisonis (Sardinia) (*CIL* 10. 7953, twenty-three *curiae*)

and in a few cities of the East:

Aquincum (*CIL* 3.10570, dedication *in onore vicanorum*)
Antioch in Pisidia (*ILS* 5081 and B. Levick, *Roman Colonies in Southern Asia Minor* [1967] 76, *vici* names imitating Rome's)
Lystra (ibid. 77 n. 3, "possibly twelve" *vici;* cf. Antioch's seven)
Poetovio (*ILS* 3302)
Sinope (*AE* 1916, 120)
Alexandria Troas (*CIL* 3.384 and 386, at least ten *vici*)

Rarely in Italy, once in Pannonia (Savaria), and at nearly thirty sites in the African provinces, the citizenry was divided into *curiae,* equivalent to *tribus* in the Latin-speaking area (Lanuvium, *CIL* 14.2114, 2120, 2126; Tarentum, *FIRA*² 1.168, the *Lex municipi Tarentini* §2; and Savaria with five *curiae, CIL* 3.4150) and to the chief gates of Phoenician cities. See at Thugga the election of *sufetes omnium portarum sententiis,* in *CIL* 8.26517, and W. Seston, *Rev. hist.* 237 (1967) 283–293. For African *curiae,* see T. Kotula, *Les curies municipales en Afrique romaine* (1968) passim, examples being, at Themetra, *AE* 1946, 234; Simitthus, *CIL* 8.14683; Rusicade, *CIL* 8.19917; Ammaedara, *CIL* 8.23261; Lambaesis, *CIL* 8.3293 and M. Leglay, *Antiquités africaines* 5 (1971) 133–135; Bulla Regia, P. Quoniam, *Karthago* 11 (1961/62) 6 f.

In the Greek East, cities had φυλαί, but how citizens were assigned to these, whether or not by neighborhood, is unknown. The population voted and on occasion assembled by tribe, κατὰ φυλήν. See Liban., *Or.* 15.76, comparing *Or.* 11.231 and 245. Two of the seven tribes of Philadelphia named after crafts are unique: ἡ ἱερὰ φυλὴ τῶν ἐριουργῶν and σκυτέων (LeBas-Wadd. 648 and 656). Otherwise, tribes bear names of gods or of members of great families, royal or imperial.

2. CRAFTS' LOCALITIES

The naming of urban districts according to the crafts concentrated in them, like some of the Roman *vici* above (even if the name lasted after the craft had gone elsewhere) was characteristic in ancient cities, beginning with the Ceramicus of Athens or the corresponding Potters' Quarter of Alexandria. We find in Rome

> *aream carruces* (*Libellus de reg. urbi Romae* p. 73)
> *forum suarium* (ibid. 83)
> *basilica argentaria* (ibid. 85)
> *porticus margaritaria* (ibid. 85)
> *Hercules olivarius* (ibid. 91, the shrine next the Olive-sellers'
>   Quarter)
> *campus lanatarius* (ibid. 93)
> *porticus fabaria* (ibid. 94)
> *forum pistorum* (ibid. 94)
> *forum vinarium* (*CIL* 6.9181 f.)
> *portus vinarius* (*CIL* 6.9189 f.)
> *Sigillaria* (Aul. Gell. 2.3.5)
> *porticus porphyretica* (*CIL* 15.7191; SHA *Vita Probi* 2)
> *scalae anulariae* (Suet., *Aug.* 72.1)
> *inter falcarios* (Cic., *Cat.* 1.4.8; *Pro Sulla* 52)
> *inter aerarios* (*CIL* 6.9186)
> *inter lignarios* (Livy 35.41.10; H. Jordan, *Topographie der
>   Stadt Rom* . . . 1 [1878] 515 n. 42)
> *inter figulos* (ibid.)

and elsewhere in Italy

clivus vitrarius sive turarius, in Puteoli (*EE* 8.365)
portus vinarius, in Falerii (*CIL* 11.3156)
forum pecuarium, in Falerio (*CIL* 9.5438)
ad Flora ad tonsores, in Velitrae (*CIL* 15.7172)

In the eastern provinces, our examples of the identification of craft and place are

τὸ ἄμφοδον Λιννφείων, in Arsinoe (BGU 110, 137, and 324; P. Teb. 321); in Socnopaei Nesos (P. Fay. 90); in Theadelphia (P. Fay. 59)

τὸ ἄμφοδον Ποιμενικόν, in Oxyrhynchus (P. Oxy. 100)
ἡ τῶν Ποιμένων λαύρα, in Oxyrhynchus (P. Oxy. 99; cf. Ποιμενικὴ 'ρύμη in P. Oxy. 43)

τὸ ἄμφοδον Χηνοβοσκῶν, in Oxyrhynchus (P. Oxy. 1634; cf. P. Oslo. 39, with refs.)

ἡ στοὰ ἣν καλοῦσι Μυρόπωλιν, in Megalopolis (Paus. 8.30.7)

ἡ σκυτικὴ Πλατεία, in Apamea (*IGR* 4.788–790)

ἡ Πλατεία τῶν σκυτοτόμων, in Settai (J. Keil and A. von Premerstein, *Denkschr. oesterr. Akad. der Wiss.* 54 [1911] 113)

ἡ Πλατεία σκυτέων, in Apollonopolis (L. Robert, *Etudes anatoliennes* [1937] 534 n. 1)

ἡ ἀγορὰ σειτική, in Tarsus (T. R. S. Broughton, *AJA* 42 [1938] 56)

τὸ ἄμφοδον σειτικόν, in el-Hamman, Palestine (*SEG* 8.43)

Timber Market, in Jerusalem (Jos., *Bell. Jud.* 2.530)
Butchers' Quarter, in Jerusalem (*Bab. Cherubin* 101a)
Woolcombers' Quarter, in Jerusalem (ibid.)
Mule-drivers' Market, in Jerusalem (*Bab. Hagig.* 9b)

In describing themselves for posterity, people often specified

both their craft and where in the city they practiced it. I give a
sampling of the abundant material, beginning with harbor
groups:

τὸ σύστημα τῶν λιμενιτῶν λινοπωλῶν of Corycus (R. Heb-
erdey and A. Wilhelm, *Denkschr. oesterr. Akad. der Wiss.*
44 [1896] 69)
οἱ σακκοφόροι λιμενῖται of Panormus (ibid.)
οἱ ἐπὶ τοῦ λιμένος ἐργ[ασταί ?], in Chios (F. Studniczka,
Ath. Mitt. 13 [1888] 170; L. Robert, *REG* 42 [1929] 37)

Rome, for obvious reasons, supplies a wealth of evidence, such
as the

faber lecticarius ab cloaca maxima (*CIL* 6.9385)
lanius de Colle Viminale (*CIL* 1.1221)
lanarii de luco Lubentinae (*CIL* 6.33870)
argentarius Macelli Magni (*CIL* 6.9183)
argentarius de Velabro (ibid. 9184)
sutor a porta Fontinale (ibid. 33914)
aurifex extra portam Flumentanam (ibid. 9208b)
mellarius a porta Trigemina (ibid. 9618)
aurifex de sacra via (ibid. 9207)
pigmentarius vici Lorari (ibid. 9796)
tonsor de vico Scauri (ibid. 9940)
caelator de sacra via (ibid. 922t)
vestiarius de horreis Agrippianis (ibid. 9972)
mercator de foro suario (ibid. 9631)

But for equally obvious reasons, we know far less about the
smaller cities of Italy. Probably their size made the fuller addresses of Rome unnecessary; but we find in Milan the *iumen-
tarii portae Vercellinae* (*CIL* 5.5872) and in Falerio the *collegia quae attingunt* (i.e. *circa forum, CIL* 9.5438). Eastern
cities, including some quite minor ones, yield

οἱ ἐργάται προπυλεῖται πρὸς τῷ Ποσειδῶνι, in Ephesus
(*CIG* 3028)

οἱ ἐν τῇ Σκυτικῇ Πλατείᾳ τεχνεῖται, in Apamea (*EE* 7.437)

οἱ ἐπὶ θερμαίας Πλατείας ἐργασταί, in Apamea (*IGR* 4.791;
cf. *CIG* 3960b)

οἱ ἐν τῇ Σεβαστῇ Πλατείᾳ, in Sura (*IGR* 3.711)

οἱ κανναβάριοι ἐν τῇ Σερβειλείου στοᾷ, in Ephesus (*SEG*
4.539 and 541b)

οἱ πορφυροβαφεῖς τῆς ὀκτωκαιδεκάτης (Πλατείας?—18th
Street), in Thessalonica (L. Robert, *Etudes anatoliennes*
[1937] 535 n.3)

οἱ ἐπὶ τῆς ἀγορᾶς πραγματευόμενοι, in Smyrna (J. Keil, *Is-
tanbuler Forsch*. 17 [1950] 59)

οἱ τοῦ σταταρίου ἐργασταί, in Thyatira (*IGR* 4.1257)

οἱ φορτηγοὶ οἱ περὶ τὸν βεῖκον, in Smyrna (J. H. Mordtmann, *Ath. Mitt*. 6 [1881] 125)

οἱ σακκοφόροι οἱ ἀπὸ τῆς ἐλαηρᾶς, in Perinthus (ibid.)

3. NEIGHBORHOODS

Large districts attracted the loyalty of their inhabitants. Harbor streets that united various worker groups (see the preceding section) on one occasion served as center for a serious
division in the population of Smyrna, pitting οἱ ἄνω against οἱ
ἐπὶ θαλάττῃ (Philostr., *Vit. soph.* 531; cf. Jos., *Vita* 66, stasis
in Tiberias involves, as one of the three factions, οἱ ναῦται καὶ
οἱ ἄποροι; the annual battle lasting several days and fought
with stones between the two sections of Caesarea [Mauretania
in the later fourth century: Aug., *De doct. christ.* 4.24.53]; and
note the hints at district-based passions in *IGR* 4.914, Philostr.,
Vit. soph. 603, and Dio Chrysos., *Or.* 45.8; for οἱ τὴν
ἀκρόπολιν κατοικοῦντες acting as a group in Pergamum, see
M. Fränkel, *Inschriften von Pergamon* [1895] 2.280 and 298).

Inhabitants of the maritime side of Pompeii constituted a borough, the Salinienses, with their own favored candidates for municipal office, their own assembly, and their own headquarters at the shrine of Hercules near the Porta Ercolanese (M. Della Corte, *Case ed abitanti di Pompeii*[2] [1954] 26; *CIL* 4.4106), and the Tiber-side fishermen at Rome celebrated their ancient games on June 8 across the river, offering their catch on the altar of Vulcan (J. Carcopino, *Mélanges J. Carcopino* [1966] 417, the *corpus piscatorum*). Higher in the city, the Subura faced the Via Sacra in an equally ancient sublimination of district hostility, the annual free-for-all over the head of the so-called October horse (misnamed "December" by Plutarch, *Moral.* 287A). The Hill-dwellers of Rome on the Septimontium seem to have had some corporate character in Cicero's mind when he speaks of them and the suburban residents (*montani* and *pagani, De domo sua* 74; *RE* s.v. *Montani* [Schur 1933] 202); they too had their separate festival each year. Another area, that of the tribe Palatina, Cicero thought of as a turbulent plague-spot (*Pro Sestio* 114). Trastevere and the Caelian were lower-class (Castagnoli, *Topografia* 139), and unspecified slums were notorious to contemporaries for their twisting alleys (Cic., *De lege agr.* 2.96; Tac., *Ann.* 15.38; Suet., *Nero* 38.1). That would be where Martial (3.30) had his *fusca cella;* but housing in general was far more expensive in the capital than elsewhere (Juv., *Sat.* 3.223 f.).

Neighbors through residence without implication of a shared craft (on those with a shared craft, see the preceding section) appear in joint activities, as *possessores circa forum* in Falerio making a contribution to the improvement of the area (*CIL* 9.5438), businessmen of the temple area of Saturn in Rome (*CIL* 1.636), the Holy Square residents in Histria (E. Popescu, *Dacia*[2] 4 [1960] 276 and 291) and the Neighborhood of the First Portal, ἡ γειτοσύνη τῶν πρωτοπυλειτῶν, in Akmonia, receiving a gift from a benefactor (W. M. Ramsay, *Cities and Bishoprics of Phrygia* [1897] 562; cf. the *portae* of Thugga, in section 1, above; and on γειτονίαι, the organizing of feasts of celebration in Rome according to that grouping, Jos., *Bell. Jud.* 7.73).

APPENDIX B

THE LEXICON OF SNOBBERY

I list here enough words and enough references for the use of these words in Greek and Roman authors to indicate the range of prejudice felt by the literate upper classes for the lower. A few special studies have been made of such words— for example, Z. Yavetz, "Plebs sordida," *Athenaeum* 43 (1965) 295–311, and O. Brabant, "Classes et professions 'maudites' chez saint Augustin . . . ," *Rev. Etudes Augustiniennes* 17 (1971) 69–81; but the most comprehensive is I. Opelt, *Die lateinischen Schimpfwörter und verwandte sprachliche Erscheinungen* (1965). I draw from these and other scattered studies without further acknowledgment.

baiulus (φορτικός): Symm., *Rel.* 3.15; Them., *Or.* 4.73

βάναυσος: Cic., *De off.* 1.150; Dio Chrysos., *Or.* 1.33; 7.108; Lucian, *Somnium* 9; Plot., *Enn.* 2.9.9

βαφεύς (*tinctor*): Dio Chrysos., *Or.* 7.117; 34.23; Firm. Matern., *Math.* 3.6.4

caupo (and *tabernarius*): Juv. 3.294 f.; Mart. 7.61; Cic., *Pro Flacco* 18; Firm. Matern., *Math.* 3.6.4

egens: egentes ac perditi (Cic., *De domo* 58; Caes., *B. G.*
7.4.3); *egentes atque improbi* (Cic., *De lege agr.* 1.22);
sceleratus latro atque egens (Cic., *Phil.*, 11.4); *corruptus
egentissimus* (Tac., *Hist.* 3.47). Compare *egestas* (*turpis*,
Virg., *Aen.* 6.276; *Octavia* 833; *deforme malum et
sceleri proclivis*, Silius Italicus 13.585; *per egestatem
abiecti in faecem vilitatem plebeiam, Cod. Theod.*
9.42.5; and linked with *infamia* and *licentia, Dig.*
47.10.35 and Tac., *Hist.* 1.46) and *paupertas*, linked
with *ignobilitas* and *ignominia* in Cic., *Tusc.* 5.15 and
29; *De fin.* 3.51
ἐριουργός (and *linteo* and λινουργός): Juv. 8.43; Orig., *C.
Cels.* 3.55; Dio Chrysos., *Or.* 34.23; *Bab. Yebamoth*
118b; Firm. Matern., *Math.* 3.6.4; and W. O. Moeller,
Technology and Culture 10 (1969) 563 f.
faenerator: Cic., *De off.* 1.151; Mart. 2.44.3; Sen., *Contr.*
9.1.12
fullo (γναφεύς): Mart. 3.59; Sen., *Ep.* 15.4; Orig., *C. Cels.*
3.55; Firm. Matern., *Math.* 3.8.7
funarius: Amm. 30.7.2
γραμματικός: Dio Chrysos., *Or.* 7.114
κάπηλος: Cic., *De off.* 1.150; Philostr., *Vita Apoll.* 4.32; *Vit.
soph.* 7.23; Art., *Oneir.* 1.23.30; Liban., *Or.* 46.10; *Ep.*
226.4; Julian, *Adv. Galil.* 238E; *Ep.* 36.422B; *Or.* 1.15C;
6.186D; Them., *Or.* 4.73; Greg. Naz. *Ep.* 2
lanista (*gladiator*): Mart. 11.66.1f.; *FIRA* ² 1.149; SHA
Trig. Tyr. 8.13; *ILS* 7846 (but cf. 5151)
lanius: Mart. 7.61; Livy 22.25.19; Firm. Matern., *Math.*
3.8.7
leno (πορνοβοσκός): Dio Chrysos., *Or.* 14.14; *FIRA*² 1.149
mango: Dio Chrysos., *Or.* 7.133
mercator (and ἔμπορος): Cic., *In Pis.* frg. 11; *De off.* 1.151;

Tac., *Ann.* 4.13; P. Baldacci, *Rend. Ist. Lombardo* 101 (1967) 273–276; S. Treggiari, *Roman Freedmen* . . . (1969) 89; C. Nicolet, *L'ordre équestre* 1 (1966) 306 and 358

mimus (ὀρχηστής): Cic., *De off.* 1.151; *Pro Quinctio* 25.78; *FIRA²* 1.149; Dio Chrysos., *Or.* 7.119; Julian, *Adv. Galil.* 238E

mulio: Cic., *Ad fam.* 10.18.3; Juv. 8.148

ναύτης: Orig., *C. Cels.* 1.63; Them., *Or.* 4.73

negotiator: Dig. 50.2.12

nummularius (and *argentarius*): Suet., *Aug.* 4.2

opifex: Cic., *Pro Flacco* 18; Sen., *Ep.* 88.23; Plin., *N. H.* pr. 6; Liban., *Or.* 58.4

παιδαγωγός: Dio Chrysos., *Or.* 7.114

pistor: Suet., *Aug.* 4.2; Cic., *Pro Roscio* 46.134; Firm. Matern., *Math.* 3.8.7

praeco: Cic., *Pro Quinctio* 12; *In Pis.* 62; *De off.* 1.150; *FIRA²* 1.148; Juv. 7.5 f.; Dio Chrysos., *Or.* 7.123

sutor: Mart. 3.59; Orig., *C. Cels.* 3.55; Liban., *Ep.* 226.4; *Or.* 29.30

τέκτων: Dio Chrysos., *Or.* 34.23

τελώνης: Dio Chrysos., *Or.* 14.14; Cic., *De off.* 1.150; Art., *Oneir.* 1.23.30; 4.42.270; Orig., *C. Cels.* 1.63; Julian, *Adv. Galil.* 238E; Philostr., *Vita Apoll.* 8.7.11

tonsor: Dio Chrysos., *Or.* 7.117; Mart. 7.61; Juv. 1.24; 10.226

unguentarius (μυρεψός): Dio Chrysos., *Or.* 7.117; Cic., *De off.* 1.150

vulgus: Hor., *Od.* 3.1 (*profanum;* cf. 3.2.21–23); Sen., *De brev. vit.* 1.1 (*impudens vel imprudens*); Tac., *Hist.* 2.21 (*pronum ad suspiciones*); 2.61 (*stolidum*); 3.31 (*inops*); 3.58 (*ignavum*); *Ann.* 2.77 (*inops*); 6.1.10 (*indoctum*); Jerome, *Ep.* 52.8 (*imperitum*); cf. similar phrases, in *Cod. Theod.* 9.42.5 (*vilitas plebeia*); Amm. 28.4.28 (*otiosa plebs et deses*); Juv. 8.44.53 (*volgi pars ultima*); Tac., *Hist.* 1.4 (*plebs sordida*); 2.61 (*fanatica multitudo*); Mart. 9.22.2 (*crassa turba*); Dio 52.8.7; and, for an interesting comparison, A. Luchaire, *Social France at the Time of Philip Augustus* (1912) 385, on the brutality and feeling of disgust shown by the upper classes to the masses.

APPENDIX C

ROMAN CITY FINANCING

Between the narrow concentration of wealth in the hands of a small local aristocracy, as it is seen in the preceding chapters, and on the other hand the thoroughly familiar picture scholars have of Roman cities well furnished with architectural amenities, there seems to be a contradiction. The contradiction can be resolved by consideration of three points.

First, we know that rich individuals were expected to contribute to their city. Though public pressure on them cannot of course be measured, it was in certain times and places demonstrably intense. They might on occasion mortgage their properties to make up the sum of an impressive gift (*ESAR* 4.667 and 670), and receive their city's thanks for giving μεγαλοψύχως καὶ πλουσίως ὑπὲρ δύναμιν (*IGR* 1.1041) or "unsparingly" (*IGR* 4.1273; *MAMA* 8.492; etc.). Even bankruptcy from such efforts is attested (Dio Chrysos., *Or.* 46.3f.); and after gifts had yielded their rewards in the form of social advancement, their beneficiaries, the benefactors of their cities, commonly relaxed their efforts (R. Duncan-Jones, *PBSR* 35 [1967] 165. In a mixed picture, the same phenomenon was detected by B. Levick, *Roman Colonies in Southern Asia Minor* [1967] 113). A. H. M. Jones, in his *Greek City* (1940) 250, is one of many scholars who acknowledge "the force of public opinion" in this regard.

Second, as the Younger Pliny's findings in Bithynia have made familiar to us, urban communities as a whole stretched to the limit their own public resources and the patriotism of their upper classes, so that choice sites were encumbered for decades with beginnings that no one had the funds to complete. At Athens, as an extreme example, the gigantic temple to Zeus waited seven centuries for its accomplishment by Hadrian; but at Cyzicus, temples to Augustus and to Persephone stood unfinished for decades, and inscriptions often refer to "baths untended by long neglect" or "a bridge in a state of collapse and disrepair by age over a long period." See *ESAR* 4.716 and 747; *CIL* 6.56; 8.1183; 9.1596; 10.772, 3344, 5917, and 7946; 11.3801; 14.2101; *ILT* 1568; and for a later period, spoliation from old buildings for new, implied or stated in *CIL* 10.1199; 14.2919; and *ILAlg.* 1.1273. We may draw a parallel with medieval cathedrals. Great Roman buildings may likewise have arisen from the most desperate effort of financing over the course of generations. And indirect confirmation lies in the often-recorded adornment of existing structures by some later donor, leading us to suppose that their initial stages were as bare as they were grandiose, and that provision for their proper embellishment or regular upkeep exceeded the community's resources.

Third, evidence exists for the cost of typical big public edifices. Let us play with figures, beginning with some place of a size like Pompeii's, and giving it the following:

theater	400,000 sesterces
curia	100,000
basilica	120,000
macellum	100,000
library	500,000
three baths buildings	400,000
	400,000
	400,000
a large temple	100,000
three small temples	60,000
	60,000
	60,000
three large decorated	50,000
fountains	50,000
	50,000
gymnasium	150,000
	3,000,000 sesterces

The evidence, from which I draw median figures for costs, comes from Africa through the researches of A. Bourgarel-Musso, *Rev. afr.* 75 (1934) 386–399, and R. Duncan-Jones, *PBSR* 30 (1962) 79–81; from Italy, idem, ibid. 33 (1965) 234–239 and 275, omitting as not representative of ordinary cities the big projects in the capital, though well attested, and the special study of *horrea*-costs at Ostia as somewhat unreliable (J. B. Becker, *Rend. Ist.* 97 [1963] 623–626); from eastern provinces, see the evidence in *ESAR* 4.787, 793, and 809; P. Collart, *Philippes* (1937) 346; and *CIL* 3.607.

To this list should be added arches (75,000 sesterces each, including statues to decorate them); honorific statues erected singly in public places (7,500 sesterces would be a typical price for each); porticoes and paving (cost according to extent);

and perhaps an aqueduct and an amphitheater. With all these and a minimal annual budget for repairs, our three million sesterces must be trebled before the urban picture familiar to us emerges in its usual fullness. What is interesting about the final total is the fact that it falls short of several known individual gifts to individual cities by their benefactors—that it may produce some one single benefactor hailed as *fabricator ex/maxima parte etiam civitatis nostrae,* at Aeclanum in Italy (*ILS* 5506)—and that it approximates the lifetime generosity of only two Younger Plinys to their home town. See Duncan-Jones, *PBSR* 33 (1965) 188, and *ESAR* 4.780. Such persons, in centers like Aquileia or Ephesus many times the size of the unit we have been imagining, would be found in correspondingly large numbers.

My calculations naturally pretend to no exactness, but they may suffice to support the rather unexpected possibility that a city's full architectural equipment might draw on the fortunes of only a very few wealthy families, expended over a generation or so. And this possibility does not require the support of other data on the yield of local taxation and endowments or the emperor's own grander munificence (on which see my article in *Harvard Studies in Class. Philol.* 64 [1959] 207-235).

NOTES

CHAPTER I

1 Marcus Aurelius, *Ep. ad Front.* p. 35 (ed. Naber).
2 Firm. Matern., *Math.* 6.31.15, and my own observation in central Turkey; for a funerary relief showing a shepherd with staff and dogs, L. Robert, *Ant. class.* 35 (1966) 383.
3 Lucian, *Ignorant Book-Collector* 3.
4 For "Shepherds' Lane" and "Shepherds' Quarter," see Appendix A2. But we also have an entire Shepherds' Village, SB 5670 (second century). For inscriptions, Robert, art. cit. 384, and in *Hellenica* 7 (1949) 155 f., 158; *IGR* 1.1116 (Egypt).
5 Firm. Matern., *Math.* 3.5.23; 4.13.7 (cf. Orig., *C. Cels.* 1.23) —as in modern Lebanon, A. H. Fuller, *Buariz* (1961) 30, or modern Turkey, P. Stirling, *Turkish Village* (1965) 223. For an interesting account of modern Greek shepherds, see J. K. Campbell, in *Mediterranean Countrymen,* ed. J. Pitt-Rivers (1963) 77 f.
6 Robert, *Hellenica* 7 (1949) 155 f., Thessaly and elsewhere; Varro, *R. R.* 2.1.16, and Dio Chrysos., *Or.* 7.13, transhumance in Italy and Greece, as in modern Syria, P. Patai, ed., *The Republic of Syria* (1956) 301 f., or medieval Sardinia, M. LeLannou, *Pâtres et paysans de la Sardaigne* (1941) 100–126. A shepherd's wandering life, Firm. Matern., *Math.* 8.6.2 and 6; *controversia pastorum* along the cattle-drifts, *ut solet,* Cic., *Pro Cluentio* 161.

7 Mounted *abiegi, Cod. Theod.* 9.30.2 f.; armed with swords, Firm. Matern., *Math.* 6.31.6; laws against stealing herds and flocks of all kinds, *Dig.* 17.2.52.3; 47.8.2.21; 47.14.1 and 3; *Cod. Theod.* 9.30.1–5; *Mos. et Rom. leg. coll.* 11.2–3; 11.6.1; 11.7.1; 11.8.4.

8 Varro, *R. R.* 2 pr. 6; Strabo 8.8.1; Dio Chrysos., *Or.* 1.52–54; 7.11; Philostr., *Vita Apoll.* 8.7.12; *Vitae soph.* 615; Lucian, *Icaromen.* 18.

9 A. Büchler, *The Economic Conditions of Judaea* (1912) 35; *Bab. Chullin* 84a.

10 *CIL* 9.2438; U. Laffi, *Studi classici e orientali* 14 (1965) 180 f.

11 *CIL* 8.23956, Henchir-Snobbeur in Proconsularis, closely similar to the regulations posted ca. 250 at Hierapolis in Phrygia (*MAMA* 4.297); cf. Robert, *Hellenica* 7 (1949) 155, the dispute concerning pasture rights in Thessaly.

12 Juv., *Sat.* 1.107 f.; Robert, *Ant. class.* 35 (1966) 384; *CIL* 8.23956.

13 Columella, *R. R.* 1.5.7; M. Schwab, *Le Talmud de Jérusalem* (1871) 1.187; cf. Jos., *B. J.* 2.125, going armed on one's travels as a matter of course.

14 R. MacMullen, *Enemies of the Roman Order* (1966) 255–268, to which many references could be added.

15 R. MacMullen, *Soldier and Civilian* (1963) 139–151; Jos., *B. J.* 2.70, implying many "fortified villages."

16 U. Kahrstedt, *Das wirtschaftliche Gesicht Griechenlands* (1954) 47; J. Day, *An Economic History of Athens under Roman Domination* (1942) 232 f. Around the date A.D. 300 on Aegean isles and the eastern coast, inscriptions from a dozen sites yield the same picture. See A. H. M. Jones, *JRS* 43 (1953) 52.

17 F. G. DePachtère, *La table hypothécaire de Veleia* (1920) 68, 91, and chart facing p. 100.

18 P. Veyne, *Mél. Rom.* 70 (1958) 216; *ESAR* 5.174; and a similar picture in A. Kahane et al., *PBSR* 36 (1968) 150–157.

19 Tabula Heracleensis 157 and the Lex Col. Gen. Iuliae 98 (*FIRA*² 1.151 and 189); *CIL* 11.419, a donation of *fundos XXI;* Plin., *Ep.* 1.4; 4.6; 5.6; SHA *Ant. Pius* 2.11; J. Carcopino, *Cicero: The Secrets of his Correspondence* (1951)

1.51; Hor., *Ep.* 1.15.45 f. To these named and specific cases of Italians with multiple holdings in Italy much indirect evidence could of course be added.

20 A ceiling placed on senators' overseas holdings: Dio 52.42.6 f.; 60.25.6; Tac., *Ann.* 12.23.1; Plin., *Ep.* 6.19; SHA *Marcus Aurelius* 11.8; provincial holdings, in Cic., *Pro Flacco* 89; *Pro Quinctio* 12; *Ad fam.* 13.69; *Dig.* 26.7.4; Sen., *Ep.* 87.7; *De vita beata* 17.2; Seneca's own holdings in Egypt, P. Bouriant 42, and probably in Galatia, W. M. Ramsay, *JRS* 16 (1926) 205; *PIR*² C 1067; F 580; *SEHRE*² 655; Amm. 27.11.1; L. Friedländer, *Roman Life and Manners* (1913) 1.113 f. To this specific evidence of the wealthy of Italy investing also overseas, much indirect evidence could easily be added.

21 Siculus Flaccus p. 152, ca. A.D. 100? (ed. Blume-Lachmann-Rudorff); cf. in Greece, Kahrstedt 85, 134, 138, 177 f.; in fourth-century Syria, P. Petit, *Libanius et la vie municipale à Antioche* (1955) 331.

22 Note the long section in the *Digest* (19.2) devoted to rentals and tenancies and indicating much litigation; the recurrence of back-dues (*reliqua, Dig.* 19.2.15; 32.91 pr.; and 32.97; Plin., *Ep.* 3.19.6; 9.37.1 f.); and Plin., *N. H.* 18.37, for a spectacular loss.

23 Cic., *De leg. agr.* 3.4.14; Plin., *Ep.* 3.19; stressing the savings made possible by *continuatio;* Petron., *Sat.* 48.3; 77.3; Hor., *Serm.* 2.6.8 f.; Sen., *Ep.* 90.39; *De benef.* 7.10; Ambrose, *De Nabuth.* 1; Jerome, *In Mich.* 2.1 (*PL* 25.1167C); Cyprian, *Ep. ad Donat.* 12.

24 Above, note 8; Plin., *N.H.* 18.35; Cyprian, loc. cit.; and Frontinus, *Controv. agr.* p. 53 (ed. Blume-Lachmann-Rudorff), with comment and modification by P. Romanelli, *Atti del Iº Congresso nazionale di studi romani* (1929) 341, 346, and H. d'Escurac-Doisy, *Antiquités africaines* 1 (1967) 60.

25 Cic., *Parad. Stoic.* 6.46; *CIL* 3.7000 (Orcistus in Phrygia, 323/326); Dio Chrysos., *Or.* 46.7; Sen., *Ep.* 90.39.

26 Cic., *Pro Milone* 74; Euseb., *H. E.* 4.26.5 (Asia, second century).

27 Cic., *Pro Caecina* 9, 20, and 22; *Pro Tullio* 7 f., 14, 18–21; *Pro Sulla* 71; for the sharp defense of one's boundaries, cf. Sen., *De brev. vit.* 3.1; *Dig.* 47.11.9.

28 Ael. Arist., *Or.* 50.105.

29 Above, note 26; compare two young men's land attacked in their absence, Greg. Naz., *Ep.* 14 (Cappadocia in ca. 370).

30 For a start, see L. Harmand, *Le patronat* . . . (1957), P. A. Brunt, *Proc. Cam. Philos. Soc.* 11 (1965) 1–20, and G. E. M. de Ste. Croix, *Brit. Journ. Sociol.* 5 (1954) 33–48.

31 P. Merton 92 (324).

32 Above, notes 6 f., 10 f.; for attacks on shepherds, presumably by persons defending crops, see BGU 759 and P. Bon. 20.

33 Slightly condensed, without ellipses shown, from P. Mich. VI 422 and 424 f. (197–199).

34 P. Mich. V 228 and 230; P. Mich. VI 421; P. Cairo Goodspeed 15; P. Oslo 22; P. Oxy. 903 and 2234; P. Tebt. 331; SB 7205; BGU 759; P. Hamb. 10; P. Ryl. 136, 141, 144 f., 151; P. Fay. 108; and *BCH* 7 (1883) 63 f. (9 b.c. in Cnidus).

35 SB 5238; P. Mich. III 175; P. Mich. V 229 f.; P. Ryl. 125, 127–130, 135, 138, 140, 142, 145 f., 150 f.; P. Oxy. 69 and 1272; P. Merton 65; P. Fay. 108.

36 P. Cairo Goodspeed 15; SB 5235 and 5238.

37 P. Fouad 29; P. Oxy. 2234; P. Milan Vogliano 74.

38 P. Fouad 26; P. Ryl. 134, 141, and 144; Basil, *Ep.* 3 (175); verdict ignored, SB 5238; BGU 908.

39 P. Tebt. 331; P. Amh. 142; P. Thead. 24.

40 P. Oslo 22; P. Thead. 18 f.; P. Amh. 78 and 141f.; BGU 22, 522, 648, and 970; P. Merton 26 line 9; P. Lon. 983; P. Ryl. 117.

41 P. Mich. VI 421; P. Bon. 20; P. Cairo Isidore 75; P. Oxy. 2233; P. Fouad 29; Juv., *Sat.* 15.27 f.

42 P. Fouad 26 (157/9): πολὺ ἐπὶ τῶν τόπων δυνάμενος; cf. P. Amh. 142, the rich τῇ ἐπὶ τόπων τυραννίᾳ χρώμενοι.

43 P. Cairo Goodspeed 15; P. Amh. 142; P. Cairo Isidore 75.

44 P. Amh. 77 and 134; SB 4416.

45 BGU 515 and 908; P. Thead. 18; and P. Lon. 162.

46 P. Wisconsin 33 (post 47), with the editors' note, and P. Hamb. 10.

47 A. E. Samuel et al., *Death and Taxes* (1971) 15 f.
48 *ESAR* 2.246, without naming the papyrus; BGU 115; M. Hombert, *Mélanges Paul Thomas* (1930) 440–450; Hombert and C. Préaux, *Recherches sur le recensement dans l'Egypte romaine* (1952) 19–21, household of 17 persons, but (p. 154) 6 persons is the average.
49 A. Calderini, *Aegyptus* 33 (1953) 363, finds the percentages of bastards varying from 1–17 percent in various documents. More data are available. In a list of 96 fully readable entries from one village in the reign of Antoninus Pius, 13 are ἀπάτορες (J. Day, *Tax Documents from Theadelphia* [1956] 120–126). In another list of names, 7 of 102 are fatherless, P. Petaus 108 (184/185). The term recurs often (BGU 26, 90, 117, 224, 447, 971; PSI 1244; P. Mich. VI 370; P. Flor. 5; P. Oxy. 2121; etc.). We may compare the implications of the term *Shethuki* in Palestine, denoting bastards as a recognized class or caste (*Bab. Kiddushin* 69a; *Sotah* 43a; etc.), and in Italy as well (*spurii, CIL* 11.1147).
50 *Sarcinator,* Serv., *Aen.* 12.13; cf. Matt. 9.16; abandoned shack an object of litigation, *Dig.* 1.8.5 f.; barley grains salvaged from dung, Büchler, op. cit. (above, note 9) 22 and 30; on exposure of children to be made slaves, below, chapter 4 n. 8.
51 *ESAR* 2.611 n.22; living expenses, ibid. 304 f.; *presbyteroi,* A. Tomsin, *Bull. Acad. roy. Belgique* 38 (1952) 127, 506, 514 f. I agree with Tomsin (and with P. Jouguet, *La vie municipale dans l'Egypte romaine* [1911] 219, and F. G. Kenyon and H. I. Bell in their note to P. Lon. 1220) that that the qualification, πόρος, means income and not registered value of property; but specifically it means income from land, as U. Wilcken, *Grundzüge und Chrestomathie der Papyruskunde* I, 1 (1912) 342 f., has shown (with Jouguet 220, against P. M. Meyer in his notes to P. Giess. 58, pp. 8 f., and A. C. Johnson in *ESAR* 2.611 n.22).
52 In addition to my own casual observations in the backcountry of Tunisia, Turkey, and over five months in a village in southwest Cyprus, and in addition to the sources cited above, notes 5 f., I have made use of H. H. Ayrout, *The Egyptian Peasant* (1963); A. Latron, *La vie rurale en*

Syrie et au Liban (1936); X. Yacono, *La colonisation des plaines du Chélif* (1955); J. Weulersse, *Paysans de Syrie et Proche-Orient* (1946); J. Lopreato, *Peasants No More* (1967); R. Porak, *Un village de France* (1943); E. Friedl, *Vasilika* (1962); P. Stirling, *Turkish Village* (1965); L. E. Sweet, *Tell Toqaan: A Syrian Village* (1960); J. Abu-Lughod, *Am. Journ. Sociol.* 47 (1961) 27 f.; P. Walcot, *Greek Peasants* (1970); J. Pitt-Rivers, ed., *Mediterranean Countrymen* (1963: articles by J. K. Campbell, I. Chiva, E. L. Peters, and P. Stirling); and P. D. Bardis, *Rural Sociology* 24 (1959) 362–365.

53 A. C. Johnson and L. C. West, *Byzantine Egypt, Economic Studies* (1949) 14–16, 19 f., 72, the old categories disappearing under Diocletian and Constantine.

54 For leases of village common, Tomsin (art. cit., note 51) 482; P. Lon. 842 (140); P. Ryl. 100 (238); etc.; arable leased, P. Teb. 341 (140/1); P. Oxy. 2141 (208); etc. For a σύνοδος τῶν βουκόλων, see P. Lon. 1170 Verso (258/9); P. Fay. 110 (94), a γραμματεύς κτηνοτρόφων; P. Hamb. 34 (159/60, an association of Shepherds with Elders (also *IGR* 1.1116).

55 Tenants of crown land, P. Hamb. 3; fishermen, PSI 901; carpenters, *IGR* 1.1155; P. Grenf. 43, ἡγούμενος γερδίων; Elders of the same trade, *IGR* 1.1122; weavers' associations in other villages, BGU 1564; P. Ryl. 189; etc.

56 Βουκόλος as a personal name, SB 4366, P. Bouriant 42 XVI, P. Teb. 867 line 188, P. Ryl. 657 and 691, etc.; Γέρδιος, in BGU 6 (cf. Tomsin p. 512); Τέκτων, in BGU 277, P. Teb. Mich. 121 R IV vii 33; etc.

57 See Appendix A2.

58 P. Bremer 63 is unique and obscure. Threats to abandon one's work are not infrequent among peasants of Egypt as elsewhere; but they appeal to the state as employer: if our obligations are increased or we are made to pay some certain tribute, we will be driven into exile and thus the state will lose taxpayers.

59 Juv., *Sat.* 15.38–46, slightly condensed. On the σύνοδος κώμης see P. Collart, *CRAI* 1943, 322 f.; W. L. Westermann, *JEA* 10 (1924) 136 f., and *JEA* 18 (1932) 23 f.

60 P. Lon. 1170 (cf. Fronto, *Ep. ad M. Caes.* p. 68 [ed. Naber], *vindemiatores* sing at their work); Westermann, *JEA* 10 (1924) 134–140; 18 (1932) 23–25; Collart, art. cit.; F. Dölger, *Antike und Christentum* 4 (1934) 253–260; on Egyptian festivals in general, see J. Lindsay, *Leisure and Pleasure in Roman Egypt* (1965) 1–61.

61 E. M. Husselman, *TAPA* 83 (1952) 69 f.; cf. above, notes 53 f., on community lands, contracts with workers, and so forth.

62 For transactions recorded "in the street," see examples in W. L. Westermann, *Aegyptus* 13 (1933) 230 col. II; P. Teb. 407; and P. Collart, *Mélanges Gustave Glotz* 1 (1932) 243.

63 H. Braunert, *Die Binnenwanderung. Studien zur Sozialgeschichte Ägyptens* (1964) 115 f., 126, 131–134.

64 Ibid., 244 f., 261 f.

65 Ibid. 150–156; cf. 247, typically 5–20 percent of village population are not farmers, a figure falling a little below the estimate of A. Calderini, *La composizione della famiglia . . . dell'Egitto romano* (1923) 24.

66 Braunert 150 f., 197.

67 A. E. Samuel, op. cit. (above, note 47) 23, describing Thebes only, but agreeing with general statements of other scholars and my own impressions for the province as a whole.

68 Braunert 163 and 174; A. Calderini, *JEA* 40 (1954) 19 f.; P. Corn. 24 (56).

69 Terminology is not our concern, but see A. H. M. Jones, *The Greek City* (1940) 272 f.; G. M. Harper, *Village Administration in the Roman Province of Syria* (1928) 46 f.; *RE* Suppl. IV s.v. Κώμη (E. Swoboda 1924) cols. 969 f.

70 J. Keil and A. von Premerstein, *Denkschr. der Oesterr. Akad. der Wiss.* 57 (1914) 79; Jones 272; H. W. Pleket, *Talanta* 2 (1970) 78 f.

71 Examples abound: G. E. Bean and T. B. Mitford, *Denkschr. der Oesterr. Akad. der Wiss.* 102 (1970) 28; LeBas-Wadd. 2463; G. Tchalenko, *Villages antiques de la Syrie du Nord* 1 (1953) 281; *IGR* 4.1666; etc.

72 Βραβευταί in *IGR* 4.1304, 1348, 1497; T. R. S. Broughton, *TAPA* 65 (1934) 213; Πρωτοκωμήτης, in Keil and Premerstein, *Denkschr. der Oesterr. Akad. der Wiss.* 54 (1911)

105; Διοικηταί, *RE* Suppl. IV s.v. Κώμη 967; *principes loci,* in Moesia, *CIL* 3.772 and 12491. But *summae honorariae* are not specifically attested for all of these titles.

73 W. M. Ramsay, *The Social Basis of Roman Power in Asia Minor* (1941) 159 f.; P. Collart, *Philippes* (1937) 280 f., a city decurion's son is a *vicus* official; cf. L. Robert, *Etudes anatoliennes* (1937) 242 f.; on absentee landowners, see the γεοκτεῖται (*ESAR* 4.638 f.), ἐνκεκτημένοι (*IGR* 4.1087), or ἐνκτήτορες (Keil and Premerstein, *Denkschr. oesterr. Akad. der Wiss.* 57 [1914] 70), as opposed to "the villagers," in inscriptions of various eastern regions.

74 Examples in Bean and Mitford 137; W. H. C. Frend, *JRS* 46 (1956) 53; for the village βουλευταί, cf. Harper 48 f., versus Jones 272.

75 *OGIS* 488.

76 LeBas-Wadd. 2505.

77 *IGR* 3.1154 and 1186; 4.889 and 1381; LeBas-Wadd. 2479; Robert, *Etudes anatoliennes* 242; Jones 272.

78 Real estate in common, *IGR* 4.1666 and LeBas-Wadd. 2463; gift to *vicus, CIL* 3.656.

79 Libanius, *Or.* 11.230; MacMullen, *Phoenix* 24 (1970) 335 f.

80 Robert, *Rev. de philol.* 17 (1943) 189–193.

81 Ibid. 193; for other *koina* of villages, cf. *RE* Suppl. IV s.v. Κώμη 964 f.; *IGR* 3.154; *OGIS* 519.

82 Tchalenko 1.51 and n.2; 127 and n.4; S. Krauss, *Talmudische Archäologie* 2 (1911) 351; and much indirect and fuzzy evidence, such as the evidence of peddlers and imported articles found in villages, etc. See further below, pp. 162 f.

83 Tac., *Germ.* 16.2, for Italy; for village *horrea,* see W. H. C. Frend, *The Donatist Church* (1952) 45, and the *paganica* of *CIL* 8.16367 f. and M. Duval and J.-C. Colvin, *CRAI* 1972, 133–172. Compare Syrian *androns,* Tchalenko 1.29, 281, and 324, and Egyptian barns, in Husselman, art. cit. (above, note 61).

84 Varro, *R. R.* 1.17.2, *pauperculi qui ipsi colunt cum sua progenie;* 2 pr. 4, *culturam agri docuerunt pastores progeniem suam;* Hor., *Epod.* 2.3, *paterna rura bobus exercit suis; CIL* 9.6374 and 10.1877 and 1918, cited in R. Clausing, *The Roman Colonate* (1925) 279 n.5; for other provinces,

ibid. 152 f., 186–189, and chap. 9 passim; Keil and Premerstein, op. cit. (above, note 70) 37 f., peasants "of the imperial
estates, where as farmers we were born, raised, and have
from our forebears dwelt."
85 H. d'Escurac-Doisy, *Antiquités africaines* 1 (1967) 67–69;
F. G. de Pachtère, *Mél. Rome* 28 (1908) 374 f.
86 On village government, see first the rich article of E. Korne-
mann, *RE* s.v. Pagus (1942) 2322 ff.; further, *SEHRE*² 325;
on the *ordo decurionum* of African villages, d'Escurac-Doisy
61; and on African *pagi,* C. Poinssot, *BCTH*² 5 (1969) 215–
258, and P. Romanelli, *Storia delle province romane dell'*
Africa (1959) 188, 197–200, and 670. *RE* s.v. Vicus (A. Van
Buren, 1958) is of little use.
87 On emperors as *patroni,* H. F. Pelham, *Essays* (1911) 296–
299; on Africa, Poinssot passim, and esp. *ILT* 1514, a
patronus pagi of Dougga thanked as *advocatus eloquentissi-*
mus; in Italy, such inscriptions as *CIL* 9.1503, 1618, 4206,
5565; 11.1947.
88 *Possessores* are sometimes no more than their name implies,
e.g. around Lambaesis, veterans settled with lands, *AE* 1964,
no. 196 (Ant. Pius); but the *possessores vici Verecundensis*
of *CIL* 8.4199 and 4205 included a magnate of a nearby
town (*CIL* 8.4194; d'Escurac-Doisy, loc. cit.; cf. above, note
51, for a parallel requirement of landed property). In Italy
and, we may add, Gaul also, we meet an *ordo possessorius*
(*CIL* 10.4863, the text obscure, but I accept the interpretation of P. Wuilleumier, *REA* 36 [1934] 201 f.) and official
village action is taken through *possessores* (*CIL* 5.5872 and
5878). Near Brixellum and Ravenna, *possessores* are prominent but distinct from the local *ordo* (*CIL* 11.15 and p. 183).
89 Village watchdogs and stonings: Apul., *Met.* 4.20; 8.17;
Liban., *Or.* 47.4; above, notes 2, 27, 32, and 41.
90 Calderini, op. cit. (above, note 65) is impressionistic and
incomplete. A much better work is feasible.

CHAPTER II

1 Sen., *Ep.* 86; Apul., *Apol.* 18.11; 88.4 and 6; Cato, *R. R.*
praef.; Cic., *De senectute* 51–60; *Pro Roscio* 15.17; Varro,

R. R. 3.1.5; Columella, *R. R.* 1 pr. 6 and 14; Juv., *Sat.* 3.166 f., 190 f.; 14.166–188; Calp. Sic., *Ecl.* 2.60; Vergil, e.g. *Georg.* 2.467, 473 f., rural honesty and piety and justice contrasted with their lack in cities.

2 Musonius 11 (ed. C. E. Lutz, *Yale Class. Studies* 10 [1947] 80–84); Dio Chrysos., *Or.* 7 (esp. 7.108); Synes., *Ep.* 148 (ed. R. Hercher, *Epistolographi graeci* p. 732); Themist., *Or.* 30 (ed. Dindorf), esp. 30.349D, 350C–351A; Liban., *Laudatio* 7; cf. Firm. Matern., *Math.* 4.19.32, on the general reputation of farmers as honest folk.

3 Juv., *Sat.* 3.67 f.; on crude, clumsy appearance, Dio Chrysos., *Or.* 31.162; 35.11 (cf. Plut., *Moral.* 57A, scorn of the peasant in his hide jacket; Mart. 7.58.8; Cic., *De off.* 1.35.129); rusticity clashes with elegance, Cic., *Phil.* 10.10.22; *De fin.* 3.14; Apul., *Apol.* 16.10; cf. his use of the words *rusticus* and *rusticanus,* always derogatorily, ibid. 9.1; 10.6; 23.5; and 70.3—just as in the *Epit. de Caes.* 37.1; 40.10, 15, and 18; 41.9; Amm. 21.10.8; 30.4.2; 31.14.5; and Firm. Matern., *De errore profan. relig.* 16.1. For a thoughtful study of the problem in the Republic, see H. Bléry, *Rusticité et urbanité romaines* (1911).

4 Clem., *Recog.* 1.9 and 62; F. Halkin, *Anal. Boll.* 81 (1963) 5; Aul. Gell., praef. 12; 13.6.2 f.; Dio 78.21.2; SHA *Had.* 3.1; Orig., *C. Cels.* 3.55; Cic., *Orator* 161 and 172; *Brutus* 258; *De orat.* 3.11.42; 3.12.46; Quint. 2.21.6; 6.3.17; 11.3.30; 12.10.53; Plin., *N. H.* pr. 6.

5 SHA *Sept. Sev.* 15.7; 19.10; Cic., *Brutus* 170 f. and 258; *De orat.* 3.12.44; *Pro Archia* 26; *Ad fam.* 9.15.2; Quint. 1.5.56; 6.3.17; 8.2.3; 11.3.30; Stat., *Silv.* 4.45 f.; J. Herman, *Bull. Soc. ling. de Paris* 60 (1965) 60, 64 f., 67–69; E. Löfstedt, *Late Latin* (1959) 39 and 53; G. Nencioni, *Studi italiani di filol. class.*[2] 16 (1939) 41–45; E. S. Ramage, *TAPA* 92 (1961) 481–494.

6 Dio 60.17.4; cf. Juv., *Sat.* 6.187 f., for Romans to speak Greek is *turpe.*

7 Cic., *Divin. in Caec.* 12.39; Lucian, *Navig.* 2; Tat., *Ad Graec.* 1; Philostr., *Vit. soph.* 578 f.; E. H. Sturtevant, *Pronunciation of Greek and Latin*[2] (1940) 37 f.

8 Illiterate Greek and Latin in back-country inscriptions is of course a common thing, but only A. Mocsy has looked closely at the phenomenon (in Moesia: *Gesellschaft und Romanisation* . . . [1970] 233 f.).

9 See for example C. Préaux, *Mitt. aus der Papyrussammlung der oesterr. Nationalbibliothek*² 5 (1956) 109; P. Oslo 32 (among thousands of illustrations that one might choose); and analysis of Coptic influence on morphology and syntax by F. T. Gignac, *Proc. XII Int. Congr. Papyrology* (1970) 141–51.

10 Strabo 13.1.25; Greg. Naz., *Or.* 2.29; ἀστικοί contrasted with ἀγροικία.

11 G. R. Driver, *HThR* 29 (1936) 172.

12 Note phrases like the *sordidum negotium* and *ruris miseriae* of farming, Columella, *R. R.* 1 pr. 1 and Aurel. Vict., *De Caes.* 39.26; κωμητικὴ αὐθαδία, *FIRA*² 3.590; and exemption from *tutela, per rusticitatem* (ibid. 2.501, Ulpian; cf. p. 511 and *Dig.* 27.1.6.19, Modestinus).

13 Ael. Arist., *Or.* 26.8, compares Rome's high buildings to mountain peaks; on the crowds there, Lucian, *Nigrinus* 29; cf. Dio Chrysos., *Or.* 7.37, on a peasant's view of a Greek city, and the humble envoys from Palestine who could hear Rome's clamor all the way from Puteoli, in M. Hadas, *Philol. Quart.* 8 (1929) 375. But Romans too complained of the noisiness of their city day and night: Juv., *Sat.* 3.236 f.; Hor., *Ep.* 2.2.79 f.; *Carm.* 3.29.12.

14 *Bab. Cherub.* 21b.

15 J. Robert, *REG* 80 (1967) 282, "from good stock, a farmer for a long stretch"; L. Robert, *Rev. de philol.* 31 (1957) 19, "He rejoiced in the harvest, . . . and suddenly departed this life in prosperity." *ILAlg.* 1.1362, *omnibus honoribus functus, pater III equitum Romanorum, in foro iuris peritus, agricola bonus; agricola optimus*, a *vilicus* of Velitrae (*CIL* 10.6592); for a bas relief, *SEHRE*² 240, and *CIL* 3.12491.

16 Epitaphs of the Greek provinces in L. Robert, *Rev. de philol.* 31 (1957) 20; 32 (1958) 54; *Hellenica* 11–12 (1960) 321, 324 f.

17 R. MacMullen, *Enemies of the Roman Order* (1966) Appendix A.

18 Ibid. 253, Apollonius of Tyana, the historicity of the incident in doubt; but perhaps for my purposes, if it is fiction, its claim to typicality is strengthened. *Dig.* 47.11.6 (Ulpian) adds confirmation, without our reaching beyond our period to Julian's findings during the shortage at Antioch.

19 Ibid. 253, Galen.

20 Sale of sparrows, Matt. 10.29. On drawers of water, cf. Firm. Matern., *Mat.* 3.9.3; 4.13.6; and 4.14.14; Ptol., *Tetrabiblos* (ed. W. Kroll) 179; and Art., *Oneir.* 1.48. For the poor tithe and corner-gleanings, see A. Büchler, *The Economic Conditions of Judaea* (1912) 31, and *Bab. Sotah* 21b, the possessor of 200 denarii "may not take the gleanings, forgotten sheaves, the produce of the corner of the field, or the poor tithe." In Italy, Varro (*R. R.* 1.53) expected to find day laborers to glean by contract.

21 Hadas, art. cit. (above, note 13) 385, and reference to "very frequent" complaints of the sort in rabbinic literature; cf. ibid. 379, and D. Sperber, *AC* 38 (1969) 165 n.9.

22 Ibid. 166 (third century).

23 Anon., *De rebus bell.* pr. 6 (ed. E. A. Thompson); Lact., *De mort. persecut.* 7.3; Liban., *Or.* 17.27—these to be added, for a later period, to the texts scattered throughout *ESAR* vols. 2, 4, and 5 (indexes, s.v. Taxes and Tithes).

24 Some examples of the argument in Jos., *Ant. Jud.* 18.274; *CIL* 8.14428; *IGR* 1.674; Sperber, art. cit. (above, note 21) 167 n.18; J. Keil and A. von Premerstein, *Denkschr. oesterr. Akad. der Wiss.* 57 (1914) 37 f., no. 10; N. Lewis, *RIDA* 15 (1968) 141; I. Stoian, *Dacia*² 3 (1959) 376 f.; P. Oxy. 488, 2235, and 2410; P. Teb. 327.

25 *R. R.* 1.17.2; cf. Julian, *Ep.* 89b.290A (ed. J. Bidez), pitying "the poor that wander about," whose poverty stems from "us who have wealth, in our insatiate avarice."

26 Disarmament after conquest: Pannonia (Dio 54.31.3), Britain (ibid. 60.21.5; Tac., *Ann.* 12.31), Gaul (Strabo 4.1.2), Egypt (Philo, *In Flacc.* 92 f.), and a general law, *Dig.* 48.6.1; for the rest of the pattern, seen for illustration in Judaea

and Egypt, for Judaea, Euseb., *H. E.* 1.5.5; Jos., *Ant. Jud.* 18.2 and 4; Tac., *Ann.* 2.42; and for Egypt, Strabo 17.1.53; Amm. 17.4.5; and S. L. Wallace, *Taxation in Egypt* . . . (1938) passim, esp. chap. 7.

27 *SIG*³ 832; Strabo 10.5.3; *OGIS* 519, *IGR* 4.598, and *FIRA*² 1.496. Perhaps this sort of appeal by humble people was what Aelius Aristides had in mind in his speech *To Rome* (*Or.* 26.65).

28 Philo, *De spec. leg.* 3.159–162.

29 *FIRA*² 1.496 (Africa); Lact., *De mort. persecut.* 23.2 and 31.3 f., of tortures applied in the empire at large; lying to cheat the census, in Basil, *Ep.* 85 (Asia in 372), and D. Sperber, *Journ. of Econ. and Soc. Hist. of the Orient* 14 (1971) 229 (Judaea of the third century); endurance of beatings, Amm. 22.16.23 (fourth-century Egypt).

30 See the works cited in chapter 1 notes 17 f., for second-century Italy; in Africa, P. Romanelli, *Atti del 1⁰ Congresso naz. di studi romani* (1929) 346, and H. d'Escurac-Doisy, *Antiquités africaines* 1 (1967) 60, on small holdings, of which R. M. Haywood (*ESAR* 4.102) and M. Rostovtzeff (e.g. in *SEHRE*² chap. 7) have almost nothing to say; for Syria, see G. Tchalenko, *Villages antiques de la Syrie du Nord* 1 (1953) 401 and passim.

31 *Dig.* 47.11.6, Ulpian; Liban., *Or.* 16.23 f.; Ambrose, *De Nabuthe* 7.35; Joh. Chrysos., *Hom. in Matthaeum* LXI–LXII (*PG* 58.591 f.); Basil, *In illud Lucae* 46C, very full and emphatic; Soz., *H. E.* 3.16; Sperber, art. cit. (above, note 24) 232 f.

32 Tchalenko 1.26 f., 312–314, 323 (first- to third-century Syria); cf. 1 (1958) plate CX.

33 U. Kahrstedt, *Das wirtschaftliche Gesicht Griechenlands* (1954) 126, 134, 138, 177 f.; cf. P. Veyne, *Mél. Rome* 70 (1958) 214, referring to a great *gens* of landowners in south-central Italy, where "the people of Saepinum called them simply 'the Neratii', as if speaking of the lords of the place" (*CIL* 9.2484).

34 Some references I have come on are: *Bab. Cherub.* 59a; *Midrash Baba Bathra* 4.7; Vettius Valens, *Anth.* p. 66 (ed.

W. Kroll); E. A. Wallis Budge, *The Paradise of the Holy Fathers* (1909) 1.162; Strabo 5.3.2, a number of Italian villages "now . . . the property of private individuals"; *IGR* 3.1020, "Baetocaece formerly owned by Demetrius"; *IGR* 4.887–893 (Ormela belonging to the Ummidii Quadrati); Liban., *Or.* 47.4 and 11 (around Antioch); Frontinus, *Controv. agr.* p. 53 (ed. Lachmann), and *CIL* 8.8280, in Africa. Note also the whole phenomenon of villages bearing a (not specifically identifiable) family's name, examples of which are the *vicus Haterianus* (*CIL* 8.23125), another whose owner says explicitly, *vicus nomine ipsius* (sc. himself) *appellatur, AE* 1913, 226; *Verecundensis* (*CIL* 8.4192 and 4199, eventually an imperial estate, *vicus Augustorum,* 8.4194)—all these in Africa; *vicus Celeris* (*AE* 1924, 147; *CIL* 3.7526), *Quintionis* (*AE* 1919, 13), and others all in Moesia (*SEHRE*² 646); *Bassiana* and *Mogentiana,* grown from villa-hamlets to cities without losing the names of their original masters, in Pannonia (*RE* Suppl. IX s.v. Pannonia [A. Mocsy, 1962] col. 672), like modern Carmiano in Italy, from the *saltus* of Carminius Vetus (*PIR*² C 436). In the Greek-speaking provinces the evidence generally predates our period, but cf. the village Quintus, R. Mouterde, *Mél. Univ. St. Joseph* 28 (1949–50) 27; L. Robert, *Etudes anatoliennes* (1937) 242 f., the village "of Charmides," who "must have been a great landowner;" and in Egypt, the κώμη Βουκόλων τῆς ᾿Αντωνιανῆς οὐσίας, SB 5670, and P. Ryl. 134, a village on a private estate, like the κῶμαι Ταυρίνου and Σινκερή (P. Fay. 38 and SB 9053; P. Strass. 78). The imperial estates formed out of great private holdings—best known in Africa and Egypt—embraced whole villages. But enough of examples to illustrate an obvious fact.

35 *Midrash Baba Bathra* 4.7, sale of a town; *IGR* 4.582 f., donation of rents; *nundinae* established in monopolized villages, R. MacMullen, *Phoenix* 24 (1970) 334 f.; assignment of labors, *CIL* 9.2828 (Uscosium, A.D. 140, *lacum purgatum operis paganorum nostrorum*); *IGR* 4.808 (note the lordly phrase, "through the help of *his own* farmers"); Greg. Nyss., *Ep.* 25 (*PG* 46.1097); and Herodian 7.4.3 f., "the servants from the

fields . . . , obedient to the orders of their lords," join a revolt.

36 K. Buresch, *Aus Lydien* . . . (1898) 111; J. Keil and A. von Premerstein, *Denkschr. oesterr. Akad. der Wiss.* 54 (1911) 105 f.; J. Zingerle, *JOAI* 23 (1926) Beibl. 31–33. Those who perjured themselves were punished by the gods with disease, loss of property, or whatever. Their affidavits to divine power, on stone, remind one of Lourdes.

37 *Bab. Baba Kamma* 80a; cf. *Sanhedrin* 1.1; Jos., *Ant. Jud.* 14.24 and *Cod. Just.* 1.9.15; A. Büchler, *The Political and Social Leaders of* . . . *Sepphoris* (1909) 5 f., 21, 25; J. Juster, *Les Juifs dans l'empire romain* (1914) 2.33 and 95.

38 R. Taubenschlag, *The Law of Greco-Roman Egypt* (1944) 373 n.64, 377 n.87; J. Modrzejewski, *JJP* 6 (1952) 239–248 passim; Plut., *Moral.* 616C and 750A. But I cannot find a modern discussion of these texts and their legal history background.

39 Some illustrative texts: *CIL* 9.2827; Suet., *Otho* 4.2; V. Arangio-Ruiz and G. Pugliese-Carratelli, *La parola del passato* 10 (1955) 449 and 467; Vitruv. 2.8.8; and discussion in J. Crook, *Law and Life of Rome* (1967) 78. On imperial estates, *praefecti* (i.e. overseers) might sit as judges of village *controversia*, *Dig.* 43.8.2.4.

40 *Dig.* 4.8; *Cod. Just.* 2.55.1 (213); cf. the prominence of arbitration in the Herculaneum tablets. For discussion of the system from the point of view of legal history, see G. Broggini, *Iudex arbiterve* . . . (1957) passim, esp. 121–123, and K.-H. Ziegler, *Das private Schiedsgericht im antiken römischen Recht* (1971) passim, esp. 16, 37, 64, and 83–86. I owe the latter reference to the kindness of Professor D. Daube; but Ziegler has not found most of the texts in literature other than the obvious legal sources.

41 *Vir bonus:* Cato, *De agr.* 145; *Dig.* 17.2.76; Juv., *Sat.* 8.79 f.; and clearest of all, Cic., *Pro Cluentio* 182, sharply contrasting a *colonus* with a "good," i.e. a respectable, man; for nobles as arbiters, Plut., *Moral.* 479E; Plin., *Ep.* 7.30; Cic., *Pro Sulla* 60; *IGR* 3.409, Popilius Caelius Lucianus κρείνοντα τοπικὰ δικαστήρια in the village territory, with the comments

of T. R. S. Broughton, *TAPA* 65 (1934) 229 f.; and *ILS* 5982 = *CIL* 9.2827 = *FIRA*² 3.509 f., Helvidius Priscus (see *PIR*² under his name). From the second century on, the inadequacies of formal courts turned people not only to episcopal jurisdiction, as is well known, but to the arbitration of military officials as well (MacMullen, *Soldier and Civilian* 62 f.).

42 Sperber, art. cit. (above, note 29) 229 and 232.

43 Varro, *R. R.* 1.16.4; transport contract of wine from Campania, *Dig.* 19.2.11.3.

44 The *vindemitores* of Pompeii (*CIL* 4.6672; cf. Matt. 20.3, forum's loungers hired for vintage); BGU 181, Alexandrians come out as tenant farmers; *CIL* 4.490, *agricolae* of Pompeii (unless they had their own farms in the suburbs); *Bab. Baba Mezia* 83b; and P. Flor. 6, immigrants to Alexandria remanded to countryside for the harvest, A.D. 205/6.

45 Above, note 44; Varro, *R. R.* 1.17.2; P. Oxy. 1631; Columella, *R. R.* 3.21.10; digging and hoeing, ibid. 3.13.12; *Dig.* 43.24.15.1; *foenisicia,* Varro, loc. cit.; wheat, P. Flor. 80 and 101, PSI 789, etc.; olives, P. Fay. 102 (Egypt); *IG* 2/3² 1100 line 7 (Attica); E. Tengström, *Donatisten u. Katholiken* (1964) 51 f. (Africa); and vines, in Optatus 5.7 (p. 135 Ziwsa), "whoever today wants to cultivate his vineyard hires a laborer for an agreed sum."

46 Suet., *Vesp.* 1.4.

47 Common practice: often attested in Egypt, e.g. P. Flor. 101, P. Oxy. 1631; more generally, F. M. de Robertis, *Lavoro e lavoratori nel mondo romano* (1963) 195 f.

48 Crook, op. cit. (above, note 39) 196; de Robertis, *Studia et documenta historiae et iuris* 24 (1958) 270 f., 274; *mercenarii* (e.g. Varro 1.17.2; *Dig.* 7.8.4 pr.) or *stipendiarii* (e.g. *CIL* 8.25902, lines 31 f.) or *operarii* (e.g. Firm. Matern., *Math.* 3.8.7; 4.14.14).

49 *CIL* 8.11824, dated on stylistic grounds to 260/270 by G. C. Picard, *Acta of the Fifth Epigraphic Congress 1967* (1971) 272.

50 *CIL* 11.600, freely translated.

51 *PRG* III 8 (fourth century, Arsinoite nome).

52 Sperber, art. cit. (above, note 29) 234, rabbinic advice of early fourth century. Cf. the fear implied in the common term for magnates, οἱ δυνατοί (*potentes*), e.g. *IGR* 4.598; above, chap. 1 note 42. Note also Orig., *C. Cels.* 3.55, referring to "the most illiterate, rustic yokels not daring to say anything at all in front of . . . their more educated masters."

53 A. H. M. Jones, *The Later Roman Empire* (1964) 994. On the range of native languages, ibid. 991–997; R. MacMullen, *AJP* 87 (1966) 1–14; and above, note 5.

54 P. Giess. 40, trans. N. Lewis and M. Reinhold, *Roman Civilization* (1955) 2.438 f. Cf. *Corp. Pap. Jud.* 156C: "They [the Jews] don't think the same way as the Alexandrians, but more like Egyptians. Are they not on a level with those who pay the poll-tax?" (i.e. Copts); and ibid. 150, an Alexandrian Greek compares the "unmixed community of Alexandrians" with the "ill-brought-up and uncultivated" Copts.

55 P. Oxy. 1681 (third century). With Αἰγύπτιος ἀνάνθρωπος (a ἅπαξ λεγόμενον) compare Cic., *De off.* 1.36.130, *agrestis ac inhumana.*

56 P. Gnomon 38 f. in *ESAR* 2.714, distinguishing among three social levels: *astikos,* Egyptian, Roman; and (sections 45–52) regulating marriage among them. Discussion by P. Jouguet, *La vie municipale dans l'Egypte romaine* (1911) 182–184; Taubenschlag, op. cit. (above, note 38) 79–83. Note that even freedmen of Alexandrians were forbidden to marry Egyptian women, P. Gnomon 83.

57 Philo, *In Flacc.* 78, on social standing (ἀξιώματα).

58 *IGR* 3.69 (Prusias, second century).

59 These slow tides, never collectively studied, are nevertheless well known. On the inflow to cities, see (as random illustrations) M. Avi-Yonah, *Israel Exploration Journ.* 12 (1962) 132, immigration to weavers' jobs in second- and third-century Scythopolis, and L. Barkoczi, *Acta arch.* 16 (1964) 296 f., in Pannonia from Septimius Severus on; for outflow, in Egypt, H. Braunert, *Die Binnenwanderung . . .* (1964) 174; in Asia Minor, W. M. Ramsay, *Studies in the History and Art of the Eastern Provinces* (1906) 335 and 357 f.; in

Syria, Tchalenko, op. cit. (above, note 30) 1.200, 290, 375, 382, 395 f., and 405 f.; from Pompeii, H. Eschebach, *Die städtebauliche Entwicklung Pompeji* (1970) 57; without area specified, *Dig.* 50.2.1 (Ulpian).

60 *CIL* 9.3088: *primus a Betifulo* (*pago*); cf. *IGR* 1.25, a villager of Athila in Syria becomes a decurion of Canatha (second century); Broughton, *Romanization of Africa Proconsularis* (1929) 33 n.92, "many individuals native to these pagi held municipal offices and priesthoods at Carthage."

61 On village office and property qualifications, note that *munera* fell only on property-owners (M. Holleaux, *REG* 11 [1898] 273; *FIRA²* 1.189), and see above, chap. 1 notes 64, 73, and 88; on city folk settling into the country, see Keil and Premerstein, art. cit. (above, note 24) 68 and 70; A. H. M. Jones, *The Greek City* (1940) 273 f.; *SEHRE²* 662, on *CIL* 3.14384, 3; Broughton 58; B. Levick, *Roman Colonies in Southern Asia Minor* (1967) 44; and W. M. Ramsay, op. cit. (above, note 59) 335 and 340.

62 Keil and Premerstein 79; *CIL* 9.1618 (Beneventum, second century); *ILS* 6377; above, chap. 1 note 71.

63 For example, P. Collart, *Philippes* (1937) 288–290; Levick 120, on Pisidian Antioch; Büchler, op. cit. (above, note 37) 35, on Sepphoris; below, note 69, on Pompeii.

64 Cic., *De off.* 1.151; *Bab. Yebamoth* 63a.

65 *CIL* 14.2408, an *archimimus* of Bovillae; 14.2793, a *negotiator sericarius* of Gabii; 9.3688, a *cervarius; SIG³* 800, evidently a big farmer of Lycosura in Arcadia, who gave "from his wealth . . . , though the present year has been one of poor harvests," like the second-century benefactor of Pisidian Antioch, who [*ex superabundant*]*i messe populo Ant. munus promisit,* W. M. Ramsay, *JRS* 14 (1924) 178; and *ESAR* 4.667–671.

66 *SEHRE²* 153; cf. also 172 and 562 f.

67 Petron., *Sat.* 75 f.—the whole a cliché? Cf. Lucian, *Timon* 22, "a catamite-slave, in favor since his boyish days," enriched suddenly by inheritance from his master; Juv., *Sat.* 1.40; and the elder Pliny's tale, *N. H.* 34.11, reinforced by

epigraphic evidence (*CIL* 1.805 with Mommsen's note) of the slave-favorite of his mistress made rich at her death.

68 Petron., *Sat.* 71; 76.10; on his passion to build up continuous stretches of land-holding, 48.3 and 77.3, with chap. 1 above, note 23.

69 Ibid. 43.6 and 57.6, as P. Veyne points out, *Annales. Economies, sociétés, civilisations* 16 (1961) 227.

70 J. Day, *Yale Classical Studies* 3 (1932) 177 f.; cf. R. C. Carrington, *JRS* 21 (1931) 112 f.; on candidates for election, Day 178 n.80; cf. A. Clodius Flaccus, three times duumvir, "one of the most important men in Pompeii," whose "interest was evidently in wine," T. P. Wiseman, *New Men in the Roman Senate* (1971) 91; and an earlier duumvir, M. Porcius, whose wine export reached as far as Bordeaux, R. Etienne, *Bordeaux antique* (1962) 98 f. On their rich houses, *ESAR* 5.253 and W. F. Jashemski, *Class. Journ.* 62 (1967) 196-198.

71 Columella, *R. R.* 3.3.2; Plin. *N. H.* 14.48-50 and 57, including some figures on appreciation of both vineyards and stocks over a decade or two.

72 Wine and cattle: Dio Chrysos., *Or.* 46.8; Vett. Val., *Anth.* 76; Büchler, op. cit. (above, note 20) 35. Wine and cereals, ibid.; Plin., *Ep.* 5.6; 8.2; 10.8. G. Rickman, *Roman Granaries and Storehouses* (1971) 172, collects evidence pointing to the involvement of first-century millionaires in very large-scale commerce (mostly of wheat) in Rome. For great wealth of a consul of A.D. 64 derived from export of wine, oil, or wheat from his Istrian estates, see A. Degrassi, *Scritti vari* 2 (1962) 965 and 969.

73 *Bab. Chullin* 84a; Marcus Aurel., *Ep. ad Front.* p. 29 (ed. Naber), *latum fundum in sola segete frumenti et vitibus occupasse, ubi sane et fructus pulcherrimus et reditus uberrimus;* and above, chap. 1, notes 8 f.

74 Dio Chrysos., *Or.* 46.5 and 7; Apul., *Apol.* 20; J. Day, *An Economic History of Athens . . .* (1942) 236, and Philostr., *Vit. soph.* 549, on Herodes Atticus; Veyne, art. cit. (above, note 69) 239, collecting many references in the poets and

Digest; Plin., *Ep.* 10.54 (of the situation in Bithynia); Sen., *Ep.* moral. 41.7; and *Dig.* 33.4.2.1, etc.

75 Luke 12.16 f.; 14.19 f.; 16.1 f.; Matt. 25.14 f.; discussion in D. J. Herz, *Palästinajahrb.* 24 (1928) 99 f.

76 Dio Chrysos., *Or.* 46.5, τῇ αὐτοῦ δυνάμει πιστεύων, ὡς οὐδενὸς ἀμφισβητήσοντος.

77 Interest rates in A. Bourgarel-Musso, *Revue africaine* 75 (1934) 408; *ESAR* 4.491 f. and 900; 6 percent on Italian land, R. Duncan-Jones, *PBSR* 33 (1965) 302.

78 Leaving aside the data of Egypt, abundant but subject to fickle Nile flooding, cf. *ESAR* 4.183 and 185, and 2.311, for 50–100 percent changes in the price of staples within a single year.

79 *SEHRE*² 498; the interpretation developed on pp. 425 f., 452, 467, 496 f. Rebuttal by a dozen scholars, e.g. F. Oertel, *CAH* 12 (1939) 264 f.; N. H. Baynes, *JRS* 33 (1943) 33 f.; and J. Vogt, *Decline of Rome* (1967) 64 f.

80 See the sources and debates for Judaea, cited by M. Smith, *HThR* 64 (1971) 17 f., and S. Applebaum, *JRS* 51 (1971) 167 f., and for Africa, by R. MacMullen, *Enemies of the Roman Order* (1966) 353 f., especially W. H. C. Frend, *The Donatist Church* (1952) 171 f. and 190 f.

81 MacMullen, art. cit. (above, note 35) 338 f.

82 Ibid., 337, quoting J. Weulersse.

83 Cf. the area of Adonis' precinct at Laodicea, defined for "booths and stalls," *Syria* 5 (1924) 333–336; the trade at Dionysopolis, W. M. Ramsay, *Social Basis of Roman Power in Asia Minor* (1941) 76 and 218; Kahrstedt, op. cit. (above, note 33) 12; Paus. 10.32.15, a fair at Tithorea in Phocis at the annual Isis-festival; and other instances cited by Mac-Mullen, art. cit. (above, note 35) 336.

84 J. Szilagyi, *Aquincum* (1956) 151, Carnuntum; *CIL* 8.3293, Lambaesis; for Seleuceia, G. E. Bean and T. B. Mitford, *Denkschr. oesterr. Akad. der Wiss.* 102 (1970) 197, "for the benefit of his fellow-villagers the dedicant erected seven rows of seats" in the stadium.

CHAPTER III

1 Tac., *Ann.* 6.27, similar to Cicero's scorn of a man whose grandfather came from Milan (*In Pis.* 62) or was, worse yet, a *transalpinus* (*Post redit. in sen.* 15); cf. the attack, however, on a client of his for origin in a *municipium* (*Pro Sulla* 22 f.).

2 Amm. Marc. 14.6.22.

3 *Phil.* 3.15, à propos the scorn felt for his client from Aricia.

4 *Ad fam.* 7.1.3.

5 Petty pride, for example, was "small-town," Dio Chrys., *Or.* 34.46, μικροπολιτῶν.

6 LSJ s.v.; but especially clear in Strabo 196, 418, and 489.

7 Dio Chrys., *Or.* 38.42; cf. 39.1; and note also the prominence of the word "great" or "greatest" in the praises of a city. On city rivalries over size, grandeur of monuments, and pomp of titles, see the sources gathered in R. MacMullen, *Enemies of the Roman Order* (1966) 169 and 185–187.

8 Many variations occur—for example, πολῖται, μέτοικοι, γεωργοί, Ἰουδαῖοι (Jos., *Ant. Jud.* 14.115, in Cyrene); οἱ ἐνκεκριμένοι καὶ οἱ τὴν ἀγροικίαν κατοικοῦντες (*IGR* 3.69, in Prusias; cf. 4.1087); ἐκκλησιασταί, πολῖται, ἀπελεύθεροι, πάροικοι (*IGR* 3.800–802, in Sillyum); citizens, Egyptians, Romans (in the Gnomon of the Idiologos, trans. *ESAR* 2.714); δῆμος and οἱ παρεπιδημοῦντες ξένοι (G. E. Bean and T. B. Mitford, *Denkschr. oesterr. Akad. der Wiss.* 102 [1970] 32, in Cotenna); *populus intra murum morantes* (*CIL* 9.982, in Compsa); *extramurani* and *intramurani* (*CIL* 11.3797 f., in Veii); and more generally, with examples and explanation, *RE* s.v. *Incola* (Berger 1916) cols. 1251–1253.

9 Dio Chrys., *Or.* 34.21–23.

10 On Alexandrian weavers, see above, p. 46, and H. Braunert, *Die Binnenwanderung . . .* (1964) 172; on Messenian τεχνῖται not registered among the citizen tribes, *IG* 5, 1.1433, comparing the apparent opposing of *incolae* to *opifices* in Sena Gallica (*CIL* 11.6211); cf. the weaver *extramurana* in Juv., *Sat.* 8.43.

11 Cic., *De domo* 33.89, "slaves, laborers, criminals, beggars,"

raked together from *tabernae;* cf. the charge of drawing support from slaves, whose foreign origins were notorious (*Pro Milone* 73; *In Pis.* 75; *De harusp. resp.* 22); but an enemy responds, Cicero himself is a mere *inquilinus* (Sall., *Cat.* 31). For Antioch, see A. F. Norman, *JRS* 48 (1958) 80, and A. H. M. Jones, *The Later Roman Empire* (1964) 723.

12 M. Guarducci, *Acta of the Fifth Epigraphic Congress 1967* (1971) 220, Neronian graffiti in Puteoli; A. Beschaouch, *Mustitana* (1968) 207.

13 Dio Chrys., *Or.* 44.1 (quoting *Od.* 9.34) and 9.

14 Plut., *Cato maior* 18.4, slightly paraphrased. Note also the use of φιλοτιμία to mean not only the ambition for honor, but munificent giving (Plut., *Cic.* 8.1; *Phocion* 31.3; Dio Chrysos., *Or.* 46.3; LSJ s.v.), even forced contributions (Plut., *Eumenes* 4.3).

15 In late imperial Rome, the grand houses of the rich, designated *domus* in the Regionaries, occupied nearly a third of the city's residential space by my calculations: 1,790 *domus* x 958m² (average area) out of ca. 1,380 ha. (P. Lavedan and J. Hugueney, *Histoire de l'urbanisme: antiquité²* [1966] 316 and 318). They held of course far less than a third of the population; and evidence suggests similar proportions earlier, if the figure for destruction in the fire of 64 can be trusted: 3 percent *domus,* the rest *insulae,* according to Ps.-Sen., *Ep. ad Paul.* 12. It is accepted by A. Momigliano, *Riv. stor. ital.* 65 (1950) 332, citing H. Jordan also. A roughly corresponding number of *domus* in Pompeii, the seven largest west of a line along the Vico di Tesmo, occupied by my calculations some 9 percent of the residential area. In all of Ostia, only twenty-two private mansions are known. See J. E. Packer, *JRS* 57 (1967) 86.

16 Compare the 140 per acre of Paris in 1856, and Toulouse with half that density in 1695 (Lavedan and Hugueney 352). In England today, "150 is considered dense, and over 250 belongs to industrial slums of only a few of our towns" (E. Jones, *Towns and Cities* [1966] 43, cf. 106–108). The best evidence for ancient densities is gathered by J. Beloch, *Die Bevölkerung der griechisch-römischen Welt* (1886) 410,

updated by Lavedan and Hugueney 350–356; but the data are not very satisfactory. Professor W. L. MacDonald (whose reading of this chapter and cautioning remarks I gratefully acknowledge) reminds me that we know the full inhabited circuit of only one excavated town, Timgad.

17 At Pompeii, streets and municipal areas by my calculations approximate 30 percent of the excavated area (doubtless less out of the total original area); at Rome, the figure is higher, close to 40 percent (Lavedan and Hugueney 316). Our maps of excavated Djemila, Lepcis Magna, Miletus, Delos and Ostia hint at similar proportions, but in too fragmentary a way for any reasonable conclusions to be drawn. But note that many cities—Pompeii, Capua, Mactar, Djemila, Lepcis Magna, Ephesus, Delos, Miletus, etc.—had more than one forum.

18 Polyb. 1.4.6.

19 Window-sill chats, G. Hermansen, *Phoenix* 24 (1970) 344; flaying a carcass, *Bab. Pesahim* 113a; day-schools, M. Della Corte, *Case ed abitanti di Pompeii*[2] (1954) 186 f., *Sema* (*ludimagister*) *cum pueris rogat* as an election demand, and H. I. Marrou, *A History of Education in Antiquity* (1956) 430; contracts: *Puteolis in foro ante aram Augusti Hordianam . . . stipulatus, vel sim.,* in Rome and Puteoli, C. Giordano, *Rend. Accad. di archeologia, lettere e belle arti, Napoli* 41 (1966) 111–114, in the 40s A.D.; cf. chapter 1 note 62; barbers and butchers, Mart. 7.61; cf. 12.59; *fullones, Dig.* 43.10.1.4 (Papinian) and W. O. Moeller, *AJA* 75 (1971) 188; permission, *Dig.,* l.c., and *CIL* 4.1096, *permissu aedilium NN occupavit,* on the archway of the amphitheater at Pompeii; for Pompeian paintings of sidewalk businesses, see E. Magaldi, *Atti dell'Accad. Pontiana* 60 (1930) 78–81; generally, on life lived in the streets, Packer, art. cit. (above, note 15) 87.

20 Individual cries, Sen., *Ep.* 56.2; clothing, *Dig.* 14.3.5.4; hawking wares, Cic., *De divin.* 40.84; *Dig.* 14.3.5.9; Mart. 1.41.3 and 9 f. (mis-cited by Magaldi 75, who however collects a number of useful texts).

21 Noise of city, above, chapter 2 note 13; complaints about

hawkers, e.g. Sen. *Ep* 56.2 and Mart. 12.57; about gamblers' quarrels "making a foul racket by snorting in through noisy nostrils," Amm. Marc. 14.6.25; about songs in the streets, Joh. Chrysos., *Hom. ad pop. Ant.* 15.1 (*PG* 49.155), in Antioch, and Aug., *Enarr. in Ps.* 84.15, in Hippo, and songs in the harbor, Tert., *Ad Valentin.* 12.9, in Carthage, and Ael. Arist., *Or.* 15 p. 377 f. (ed. Dindorf), in Smyrna.

22 *Tabula lusoria* in the paving of fora and other public spaces of Philippi, Rome, Timgad, Lepcis Magna, etc.: P. Collart, *Philippes* (1937) 362; C. Courtois, *Timgad* (1951) 31; and D. E. L. Haynes, *Archeological and Historical Guide to . . . Antiquities of Triopolitania* (1959) 86; gaming tables in the streets, D. Levi, *Antioch Mosaic Pavements* (1947) 293 f. (with full refs.) and 329 f.; and election slogans in Pompeii by dicers and checker-players, Della Corte, op. cit. (above, note 19) 72 and 232.

23 For example, Dio Chrysos., *Or.* 9.22, a team of horses kicking each other in Corinth draw "a great throng" of watchers; compare, in fourth century B.C. Athens, the crowd drawn by a quarrel in the agora, Hyperides, *In Athenog.* 12, or Lysias, *In Sim.* 27: after four years, one can still produce 200 witnesses to a drunken street fight. Note the ease of getting witnesses assumed in the Lex Col. Gen. Iuliae, *FIRA²* 1.187 (no more than 20 allowed), and the *tanta multitudo* to hear Verres' trial, Cic., *In Verr.* 1.1.4.

24 *Dig.* 14.1.1 pr. (Ulpian).

25 I quote J. Crook's words, *Law and Life of Rome* (1967) 208.

26 Again I quote Crook, p. 243, and W. W. Buckland also, *Main Institutions of Roman Private Law* (1931) 320, though the two are somewhat at odds over whether real security was actually rare or not.

27 *Dig.* 12.2, especially 12.2.2 (Paulus), *iusiurandum . . . maiorem habet auctoritatem quam res iudicata;* 22.5.3.5, *nam quidam propter . . . lubricum consilii, alii vero propter notam et infamiam vitae suae non sunt ad testimonii fidem.*

28 E.g. *Dig.* 2.13.10.1, an *argentarius'* books are in effect public.

29 *Caveat emptor* underlies *Dig.* 4.4.16.4 (Pomponius); cf.

19.2.22.3, "In buying or selling it is naturally permissible to buy for less what is worth more or to sell for more what is worth less, and thus in one's turn to outsmart and be outsmarted; and similarly also in leasing and hiring, it is legal." On epitaphs, assertions of a *negotiator*'s *fides* and *probitas* or life lived *sine fraude* are quite common; see e.g. *CIL* 1.1210; 6.9222 and 9663; 8.11824; 9.2029 and 4796; 13.1906 and 2018; *ILAlg* II 820; *Epigraphica* 29 (1967) 46.

30 Stoning at Athens (Philostr., *Vit. soph.* 526; Lucian, *Demonax* 11), Iconium (Acta apost. 14.5), Ephesus (Philostr., *Vita Apoll.* 1.16), Smyrna (ibid. 4.8), Alexandria (*Expositio totius mundi* 37; Euseb., *H. E.* 6.41.3; 7.11.13; Liban., *Or.* 14.38), Pompeii (Tac., *Ann.* 14.17), Rome (ibid. 14.45; Cic., *In Verr.* 2.119; *De domo sua* 12; SHA *Julianus* 4.3; App., *B. C.* 2.18.126; 5.8.67 f.), Hypata in Thessaly (Apul., *Met.* 1.10; cf. 10.6), Larissa (ibid. 2.27), Parium (Lucian, *Peregrinus* 15), Abonoteichus (idem, *Alex.* 45), Olympia (idem. *Peregrinus* 19), Prusa (Dio Chrysos., *Or.* 46.11), Jerusalem (Acta apost. 7.58), and Antioch (Liban., *Or.* 1.209).

31 Lucian, *Dial. of the Dead* 375.

32 Tac., *Ann.* 14.45; Amm. Marc. 14.7.6; Soz., *H. E.* 7.14; Ambrose, *Ep.* 40.13; Liban., *Or.* 19.27; Dio Chrysos., *Or.* 46.11; *Expositio totius mundi* 37; App., *B. C.* 2.17.126 and 5.8.67.

33 P. Garnsey, *Social Status and Legal Privilege* . . . (1970) 191, refers to Petron., *Sat.* 21 and *Dig.* 9.2.4 (add 48.7.4), along with many Republican texts; for the danger of deserted streets, see Suet., *Aug.* 43.1; on help from servants in rural settings, see above, chapter 1 note 27.

34 See the excellent third chapter of T. P. Wiseman, *New Men in the Roman Senate* (1971), adding Cic., *Post redit. ad Quir.* 3; *De harusp. resp.* 56; *Pro Cnaeo Plancio* 21; Plin., *Ep.* 1.18; and Plut., *Moral* 448E.

35 Appendix A3.

36 In Rome, the Palatine in the late Republic was a choice section and became more so in the Empire, till the palace almost monopolized it; in Alexandria, the Brucheion in the third century had been "for long the residence of the aris-

tocracy" (Amm. Marc. 22.16.15), and census lists suggest concentrations of the well-to-do in sections of other Egyptian towns (MacMullen, *Soldier and Civilian* 109). In Timgad, "the southwest section was apparently the aristocratic quarter of town," to judge from the fine houses. Cf. C. Courtois, *Timgad* (1951) 50. At Pompeii, though the Via di Mercurio "by the elegance of its houses, appears to have been the most aristocratic of the whole city, with only very few shops on the outside" (M. Della Corte, *Case ed abitanti di Pompeii*[2] [1954] 34), there is no clear pattern of rich residential versus slum. None appears clearly in Ostia, either. See R. Meiggs, *Roman Ostia* (1960) 142. Slums certainly suggest themselves in the plans of the eastern parts of Delos, though taking us outside of our period, and in unhelpful mentions for Rome (Appendix A3).

37 Caracalla had to divide the Alexandrian sections by walls (Dio 78.23.3), but that was because he had virtually declared war on the city. For the mechanical naming of precincts by letter or number elsewhere, see Appendix A2, Thessalonica; *SEG* 2.839; addresses such as "Block Eight in Ward Beta" at Antinoopolis (Pap. Th. Reinach 49, lines 2, 18, etc.); and the implications in the wording of SB 8026, κηρύσσων πλινθίδος ἐν σέλισιν. House numbers are rarer still. I know only those cited in *Libyca* 7 (1959) 295 figs. 66 f. At Emporiae in Spain in 195 B.C., the earlier Greek settlers are found walled off from the natives (Livy 34.9.1) and similar physical features of separation can be seen where Roman settlers intruded on the scene, for example at Salona (a wall dividing the *urbs nova* from the *urbs vetus:* J. J. Wilkes, *Dalmatia* [1969] 224). The coalescing of a Roman military settlement (often abandoned by troops and filled up with civilians) plus its civilian *canabae,* and a pre-existing native settlement, produced an architecturally divided city, as can best be seen outside our area of study, in Algiers, for instance, or Germany; but cf. J. Fitz, *Gorsium* (1970). The subject of how colonists blended into a prior population and how they got along with the "old inhabitants," *veteres* (as we find them at Nola, Clusium, etc.; cf. E. Gabba, *Athenaeum* 29 [1951] 235, and their equivalent in Pompeii: Cic.,

Pro Sulla 60 f.), and the social condition of *conventus civium Romanorum,* invite a synthetic study which I cannot attempt here.

38 At Lambaesis, a *cuneus* was reserved for each *curia* (*CIL* 8.3293); at Rusicade also (*CIL* 8.19917). In the city theater, places were reserved for the six φυλαί at Ephesus (*Forschungen in Ephesus* 2.202 f.) and those of Stobi (B. Saria, *JOAI* 32 [1940] Beibl. cols. 32 f.) and of Athens (*DE* s.v. Curia col. 1396).

39 Baths: Liban., *Or.* 11.249, and T. Kotula, *Les curies municipales en Afrique romaine* (1968) 32; reunion hall, *CIL* 8.17906; *iuniores tribus* or *inventus curiae* (opposed to *seniores*), *DE* s.v. Curia 1398 and Liban., *Or.* 5.43 f.; officials and banquets, Kotula 88, 114, and 122; M. LeGlay, *Antiquités africaines* 5 (1971) 134 f.; official funerals for members, Kotula 126 f. and LeGlay 135.

40 For example, the Augustales enjoyed *proedria* at Aquincum and Philippi, see J. Szilagyi, *Aquincum* (1956) 151, and P. Collart, *Philippes* (1937) 269; and the same groups also received special awards at Volceii (*CIL* 10.415), Spoletum (*CIL* 11.4815), and elsewhere.

41 Senate's banquets in Rome, Aul. Gell. 12.8.2; Fronto, *Ep.* 2.7 p. 292 (ed. Naber); Dio 60.7.4; Suet., *Calig.* 17.2; and *Aug.* 35.2, the senate's *epulandi publice ius.* For village banquets, see above, chapter 1, notes 59 f. and 80 f. At Ferentinum a decurion's bequest to pay for food and drink to the triclinia of the curia, but an extra portion to the fellows *in triclinio meo,* implies fixed assignments to banquet groups (*CIL* 10.5853), explaining the otherwise mysterious *tricliniares* making a gift in *CIL* 9.4894.

42 Greek city voting tribes: W. H. Buckler, *JHS* 56 (1936) 78; *DE* s.v. Laodicea 376; A. H. M. Jones, *The Greek City* (1940) 335. Cf. other groups of roughly similar size, like the *pagus Urbulanensis* in Pompeii, Della Corte, op. cit. (above, note 19) 304, and perhaps some of the ἄμφοδα of larger Eastern cities (*SEG* 8.44; *IGLS* 1261; etc.). At Side, the four quarters were large enough to have their own *gerousiai.* See J. and L. Robert, *REG* 64 (1951) 193.

43 Twelve φυλαί at Ancyra, *IGR* 3.208; ten *curiae* at Lambaesis,

LeGlay, art. cit. (above, note 39) 134; seven *vici* at Ariminum, R. P. Duncan-Jones, *Historia* 13 (1964) 204; for size,
ibid., and Kotula, op. cit. (above, note 39) 63 f. For funeral
regulations in an African city, see *CIL* 8.14683 and Kotula
122 and 126.

44   See Appendix A1; for shows offered *vicatim*, Suet., *Aug.*
43.1. Cf. *CIL* 11.4815 (Spoletum), funds given to *magistri
vicorum, ut ex reditu* . . . *eodem die in publico vescerentur,*
and votive statues of thanks set up *vicatim,* Cic., *De off.*
3.80, and Plin., *N. H.* 33.132.

45   For *iuvenes vici,* see S. Panciera, *Archeologia classica* 22
(1970) 159 f.; for slaves joining in cult acts at Capua, *CIL*
1.681.

46   Della Corte, op. cit. (above, note 19) 255 and 286, the names
of the regular four *vicomagistri* painted at Pompeian *com-
pita.*

47   *CIL* 4.171, 193, 204, 367, 370, 440, 852, etc.—*vicini* urge
support of a candidate. The study of street loyalties lies at
the heart of Della Corte's whole fine book.

48   See Appendix A2, and *CIL* 15.7172, as the address given for
the return of property (a runaway slave) at Velitrae. Cf.
CIL 4.743, election support by *tonsores* at Pompeii.

49   Vitruv. 7.9.4; Varro, *R. R.* 3.16.23; S. B. Platner, *A Topo-
graphical Dictionary of Ancient Rome* (1929) 578; *ESAR*
5.224 n.17; Panciera, art. cit. (above, note 45) 135 f. Compare
the dandies' section of Capua, the Seplasia, a *forum Capuae,
in quo plurimi unguentarii erant* (Festus 317.340; Cic., *Pro
Sestio* 19; *In Pis.* 25).

50   In Pompeii, note the locations I 5.2 f.; 7.4; 7.7; III 10b–c;
11b; VI 1.14; 2.7; 2.26; 16.8, 13, 29, and 31; on the Via
dell'Abbondanza, Della Corte 232–235; in Cisalpina, P.
Tozzi, *Athenaeum* 49 (1971) 155 f. In the northwestern
provinces there are many similar indications: I. A. Rich-
mond, in *The Civitas Capitals of Roman Britain,* ed. J. S.
Wacher (1966) 84; A. Grenier, *Manuel d'archéologie* 6, 2
(1934) 694 n.2; E. Will, *Gallia* 20 (1962) 85; *Gallia* 24
(1966) 497; W. Lung, *Kölner Jb.* 4 (1959) 53; R. M. Swoboda, *Helvetia archeologica* 2 (1971) 8; and E. M. Wight-

man, *Roman Trier* (1970) 91. Most of this evidence shows us potteries and other industries relegated to the edges of cities, for quite natural reasons.

51 For jewelers and the like, see Panciera, art. cit. (above, note 45) 135–137; for commerce in clothing, *CIL* 6.956 and *ESAR* 5.224 n.17.

52 Traders near gates of Aquincum, J. Szilagyi, *Helikon* 6 (1966) 662; drovers at Milan, *CIL* 5.5872; σακκοφόροι ἀπὸ τοῦ Μετρητοῦ in Cyzicus, J. H. Mordtmann, *Ath. Mitt.* 6 (1881) 125; ὠμοφόροι ἐν τῇ Σιτικῇ at Tarsus, T. R. S. Broughton, *AJA* 42 (1938) 56; and workers at the harbor, Appendix A2.

53 Complaints: *Dig.* 8.5.8.5; exile of tileries by town law, *FIRA*[2] 1.184; smithies, Jos., *Bell. Jud.* 5.331; tanneries, J.-P. Waltzing, *Etude historique sur les corporations professionnelles chez les Romains* 1 (1895) 218; Juv., *Sat.* 14.201–204; *ESAR* 5.260 f.; Firm. Matern., *Math.* 3.8.7 and 3.10.8; Art., *Oneir.* 1.51 and 2.20.

54 Οἱ ἐξωπυλεῖται discussed by H. C. Youtie, *TAPA* 71 (1940) 652–657; cf. Vett. Valens 68.15 and Firm. Matern., *Math.* 3.9.3 and 4.13.7.

55 A. Büchler, *Studies in Jewish History* (1956) 234; cf. S. Krauss, *Talmudische Archäologie* 2 (1911) 255, and the like emphasis on purple-fishing at Bulis in Boeotia, Paus. 10.37.3.

56 On fishing, Strabo 14.2.21 and *SEG* 1.329 (Peuce); on special products of towns, Strabo 8.7.5 and 11.2.17, with a vast body of well-known material scattered through *ESAR*.

57 A few references that support this I have gathered casually, though with keen interest, in *The Islamic City: A Colloquium,* ed. A. H. Hourani and S. M. Stern (1970), where the importance of crafts-quarters appears at pp. 44, 58 f., 160 f., 172, and 197; further, M. Lapidus, *Middle Eastern Cities* (1969) 49–51 and 86; R. LeTourneau, *Fez in the Age of the Marinides* (1961) 20 f., 51, 71, 84, 86, 88 f.; G. Rudé, *The Crowd in the French Revolution* (1960) 15; and the article often cited (faute de mieux, I would say) by G. Sjoberg, "The Preindustrial City," *Am. Journ. Sociol.* 60 (1955) 439.

58 On peddlers, see above, note 20. The ubiquity of small shops
    can only be proved from the marble plan of parts of Rome
    and excavation maps now available for Pompeii and Ostia,
    the former yielding 26 bakers and about 200 *cauponae* and
    thermopolia, the latter yielding over 800 shops of various
    sorts (J. E. Packer, *JRS* 57 [1967] 84 f.). A. Boethius as-
    serted that cities of Greek tradition differed from Roman in
    the separation of commercial and residential sections (in his
    Roman and Greek Town Architecture [1948] 15 f. and in
    the *Proc. 2nd Int. Congr. Class. Studies . . . 1954* [1958]
    4.92), but, though this view is often cited, it seems to me
    to rest on no firm evidence. Outside of Italy, the whole
    question is at present too obscure for dogmatism.

59 The entire process invites a little more study. For a start,
    see *ESAR* 5.255; C. Giordano, *Rend. Accad. di archeologia,
    lettere e belle arti,* Napoli 41 (1966) 111–114, with refer-
    ences; M. Talamanco, *Mem. Accad. naz. dei Lincei* 6 (1955)
    105, 113–120, and 138–146; D. E. L. Haynes and P. E. D.
    Hirst, *Porta Argentariorum* (1939) 7 f.; Cic., *Ad fam.*
    10.32.3, a *circulator auctionum* in Hispalis, Spain; *Pro
    Quinctio* 25, a *praeco* working "at the Licinian atria and the
    market entryways" in Rome; *De lege agr.* 1.7, *atria auction-
    aria;* Plin., *N. H.* 34.11; S. Lieberman, *Greek in Jewish Pal-
    estine* (1942) 145; *RE* s.v. Praeco (Schneider 1953) cols.
    1198 f.; and in the Greek provinces, Philostr., *Vit. soph.* 603;
    P. Beatty Panop. 2 line 137; Dio Chrysos., *Or.* 7.123; and
    Lucian, *On Salaried Posts* 23.

60 On *collegia* (or however titled) there is surprisingly little in
    English: S. Dill, *Roman Society from Nero to Marcus Aure-
    lius* (1905) 251–286; R. Meiggs, *Roman Ostia* (1960) 311–
    336; MacMullen, *Enemies of the Roman Order* 173–179; but
    in other languages, the very useful F. Poland, *Geschichte des
    griechischen Vereinswesen* (1909); M. San Nicolo, *Aegyp-
    tisches Vereinswesen* (1913–1915); and that truly magnifi-
    cent work of scholarship, J.-P. Waltzing's (cit. above, note
    53). Many of the references to primary sources used below
    are taken from these works.

61 Members not of the craft, Waltzing 1.352 f.; ὁμότεχνον, *DE*

s.v. Lanarius 362 (rare): συντεχνία common, Poland 122; Pompeian *lignari* (*muliones*, etc.) *universi*, Waltzing, 1.169.

62 For the image makers, see Acta apost. 19.24 f.—just as the entire Sigillaria in Rome could be given over to the production of images (Schol. to Juv., *Sat*. 6.154). For other illustrations of economic interests at work, see Waltzing 1.190 and 3.526 f.; P. Tebt. 287; and Poland 410. The nineteenth-century inscription is quoted from *Apollo, Sept*. 1967, p. lvi.

63 For another grand clothing *macellum,* see the plan in L. Leschi, *Djemila* (1953).

64 For *fabri soliarii baxiarii* at Rome in a guild of at least three *centuriae,* see *CIL* 6.9404; *caupones* at Iol Caesarea, *CIL* 8.9409; *tabernarii* at Rome, *CIL* 6.9920; οἱ σκηνεῖται at Ilium, LeBas-Wadd. 1743n; and κανναβάριοι at Ephesus, *SEG* 4.539 and 541b.

65 Crafts' festivals were honored, e.g. J. P. V. D. Balsdon, *Life and Leisure in Ancient Rome* (1969) 75 and 372 n.64, and Waltzing 1.199; reserved seats, *CIL* 6.10099 (Rome) and *IGR* 4.1414 (Smyrna); cf. in the odeon at Melos, οἱ νεανίσκοι, *IG* 12, 3.1243; guilds as public benefactors, Waltzing 4.567 f. and *JOAI* 26 (1930) Beibl. col. 51 f.

66 To MacMullen, *Art Bull*. 46 (1964) 445 n.52, add SHA *Aurelianus* 34.4; M. E. Blake, *Mem. Am. Acad. Rome* 17 (1940) 97 n.109; J. Szilagyi, *Helikon* 6 (1966) 662; for a picture of carpenters parading, see H. Gummerus, *Jb. deutsch. arch. Inst*. 28 (1913) 86, and plate 12 of A. Burford, *Craftsmen in Greek and Roman Society* (1972). Guilds were often singled out as separate units of the population for public honors and distributions, MacMullen, *Enemies* 175.

67 Poland 441 f., ἀνακήρυξις or ἀναγόρευσις of decrees.

68 Della Corte, op. cit. (above, note 19) passim; MacMullen, *Enemies* 175–177; Waltzing 4.107 f.; Athan., *Hist. Arian*. 81; guild support of a pretender, H. Seyrig, *Annales arch. Syrie* 13 (1963) 161 and 163.

69 Use of prefixes like ἱερός and ἱερώτατος is common in Greek-speaking cities, the equivalent very rare in Latin areas. See generally G. Forni, *Mem. Accad. naz. dei Lincei*[8] 5 (1953) 68. A factor to be remembered is the cult activities of almost

all crafts associations, see below, p. 82. For the examples of titles cited in the text, see *SEG* 7.827; C. Humann, C. Cichorius et al., *Altertümer von Hierapolis* (1898) 85, cf. 50, 114, 174; F. W. Hasluck, *JHS* 24 (1904) 32; Poland 169 f., 562; *CIG* 9179; and *CIL* 6.404.

70 Imitation of municipal organization could be illustrated in many ways: the census of members called as a group *plebs, populus,* δῆμος; their division into voting groups called *curiae, centuriae,* etc.; their officials' titles, *curator, viator, aedilis,* γραμματεύς, etc.; the terminology of their decrees (Waltzing 1.376 f., Poland 334, 424 f. and 437 f.); receipt of *summa honoraria,* awarding of golden wreaths (Poland 425) and *proedria* (ibid. 436; W. M. Ramsay, *The Social Basis of Roman Power in Asia Minor* [1941] 170).

71 *Amici subaediani, CIL* 10.6699; *convivae marmorarii, CIL* 10.7039; cf. a συμβίωσις τῶν χαλκέων, *CIG* 3639 *add.* (Sigeion, Mysia); *sodales aerarii, CIL* 6.9136. These embody common words: compare a φειλιακόν, *MAMA* 3.58, 780, and 788; the φίλοι ἄνδρες of *IG* 2/3².1369 and the *amicitia Herculaniorum* of Venafrum, *CIL* 10.4850. For *sodales* and *sodalicia,* see for instance the *lanarii carminatores sodales,* in Tozzi, art. cit. (above, note 50) 153, and the *fratrium* of *CIL* 11.3614 and the *fabri fratres* of *CIL* 5.7487.

72 On συμβιωταί, *convivae, convictores, comestores,* etc., see Waltzing 1.323 n.2 and Poland 50 and 53 f.

73 At Ravenna, *CIL* 11.126 (typical, and sometimes a *schola* and *templum* are identical, as in *CIL* 10.1578; cf. Waltzing 1.226); at Pompeii, see the locations I 8.8; VI 8.12 f.; VI Occ. 1; and VII 1.38, for use of *cauponae* as *scholae.* For special *scholae* of Porters, etc., see W. O. Moeller, *Historia* 19 (1970) 84 n.2. For other *scholae* of some luxury, cf. Szilagyi, art. cit. (above, note 52) 661 f.; *RE* Suppl. bd. 9 s.v. Pannonia (Mocsy 1962) 604; Waltzing 1.210–230; for the word *house* meaning *association,* Waltzing 1.521 and L. Robert, Ἀρχ. ἐφ. 1969, 8 f.

74 The complaints about *cenae collegiorum* occur in Varro, *R. R.* 3.2.16; about drinking, in Cyprian, *Ep.* 67.6.2 and Philo, *In Flacc.* 4; cf. idem, *Treatise of Cherubin* 2.27 f., and the well-known *seribibi* of Pompeii, *CIL* 4.575.

75 *CIL* 14.3323; *SIG*[3] 1109; *IG* 2/3².1369; *CIL* 12.4393.
76 *CIL* 14.2112, condensed without my showing the gaps fully.
77 Societies with their own burial plots: *IG* 12, 1.937; *SIG*[3] 1116; *CIG* 9179; *CIL* 5.4483; 10.5647; Tert., *Ad Scap.* 3; and *Bab. Nazir* 52a. For the predominant importance of the banquet itself, see Waltzing 1.323. For their luxurious setting, idem. 1.229 f.
78 Mart. 4.61.3; cf. Waltzing 1.520; *CIL* 8.10890 (Cuicul); and the Dinner Club of φιλόλογοι ἄνδρες at Alexandria, Strabo 17.1.8.
79 *Cod. Just.* 8.46.3 (227) and 4 (259).
80 Hor., *Sat.* 2.2.52; Cic., *Ad Att.* 1.19.8; Sall., *Cat.* 5.2 and 4; 13.4; Ps.-Sall., *Ep.* 1.5.5 f.
81 Sall., *Cat.* 39.5; for earlier instances of these dire rights, Val. Max. 5.74 and 5.83.
82 Quint. 6.3.64.
83 Dio Chrysos., *Or.* 34.16 and 21, records a split between the two ages, the only case I know of. For fractious youth organizations, see *Dig.* 48.19.28.3 (Callistratus); W. O. Moeller, *Historia* 19 (1970) 87; and MacMullen, *Enemies* 338.
84 On age associations, see Jones, op. cit. (above, note 42) 224–226; D. Magie, *Roman Rule in Asia Minor* (1950) 857–859 (showing *gerousiae* with memberships of 71, 96, and 309+); Poland 88–99; and M. Jaczynowska, in *Recherches sur les structures sociales dans l'antiquité classique,* ed. C. Nicolet (1970) 265–274.
85 Panciera, art. cit. (above, note 45) 160; LeGlay, art. cit. (above, note 39) 135; *DE* s.v. Curia 1398; *ILS* 6271; *CIL* 8.15666 f.; 15669; 15721; 22901; *ILAfr.* 195; *CIL* 10.5853; 14.2635. The texts contain many obscurities.
86 *ILS* 6271. A study is overdue, incidentally, on the role and status of women, who appear in this text typically, almost by inadvertence. What is the *curia mulierum* of *CIL* 14.2120, the *collegium mulierum* of *CIL* 6.10423, or the γυναικεία σύνοδος of Alexandria, C. C. Edgar, *JEA* 4 (1917) 253 f.? What is implied in the separate mention of women in distributions, e.g. in S. Mrozek, *Epigraphica* 30 (1968) 159 n.2, and *CIL* 5.2072 and 9.4697; *IG* 12, 5.663 and 667?
87 Poland 287.

88 *CIL* 5.815; 8.9409; on Mercury for traders', Mars for veterans' *collegia,* see Waltzing 1.198 f.

89 Being no expert on Roman religion, I can only conjecture that differences in ritual survived the process of cult amalgamation into the hyphenated gods so often met with in the empire. That would explain such groups as the Dionysiac σπεῖρα 'Ρωμαίων in Tomi (Poland 84), the Βακχεῖον 'Ασιανῶν in Perinthus (ibid.), or the 'Αφροδισιασταὶ Σύροι in Nisyros (ibid. 190).

90 Ibid. 175 and 183; cf. the analogy of the pan-Hellenic cult centers, disproportionately honored and endowed by the cities of Magna Grecia.

91 This is the reasonable but unsupported conjecture of G. La-Piana, *HThR* 20 (1927) 217 f., for Rome; for other cities, evidence is also lacking.

92 In Rome, the Transtiberine Jews in Augustus' reign numbered 30–40,000, the other sections (e.g. the Campenses of Campus Martius, *CIL* 6.29756, and Suburenses, *CIG* 6447) being much less populous. See in general H. J. Leon, *The Jews of Ancient Rome* (1960); S. Collon, *Mél. Rome* 57 (1940) 74–86, with map; and J. Juster, *Les Juifs dans l'empire romain* (1914) 1.414 f. The last-cited covers the Jews in other localities very thoroughly, 1.208 and 414–447. Cf. Acta apost. 6.9 for the Cyrenaean etc. synagogues in Jerusalem, the Tarsians (or *tarsicarii?*) in Jerusalem (*Bab. Megillah* 26a), Tiberias, and Lydda (ibid., I. Epstein's note *ad loc.*); on the Antioch community, C. H. Kraeling, *J. Bibl. Lit.* 51 (1932) 136–143, and G. Haddad, *Annales arch. Syrie* 1 (1951) 28; at Oxyrhynchus, the ἄμφοδον 'Ιουδαικόν, P. Oxy. 335; on the Puteolan community, *RE* s.v. Puteoli (M. W. Frederiksen 1959) 2053. R. Calza, *Rend. Pont. Accad. romana di arch.* 37 (1964–1965) 157, conjectures that there was a similar Christian section at Ostia.

93 M. Schwab, *Le Talmud de Jérusalem* (1871) 1.147.

94 *Bell. Jud.* 2.124 f.

95 *CIG* 3408; *SEG* 2.871; 848, πολίτευμα Λυκίων, cf. πολίτευμα τῶν Φρυγῶν in Pompeii, *IG* 14.701; in Spain, the Malacan Syrians gathered under a patron and president, *IGR* 1.26, and the *sodalicium Bracarorum* in Pax Iulia, *AE* 1956, no.

254. For aliens' sections, see the ἄμφοδον Αὐαρηνῶν of *SEG* 2.839 (a tribal grouping like the *Numidae qui Mascululae habitant, CIL* 8.15775) and the *compitum* of Daphnae traders in Puteoli, Frederiksen, art. cit. (above, note 92) 2049.

96 Cf. at Napoca in Dacia, the *Asiani* and *Galatae consistentes* (*CIL* 3.870 and 860, with the *collegium Galatarum* at Dacian Germisara, *CIL* 3.1394), comparing Eutropius 8.6 on Trajan's importation *ex toto orbe Romano infinitas copias hominum ad . . . urbes colendas.*

97 Trans. N. Lewis and M. Reinhold, *Roman Civilization* (1955) 2.196 f.; cf. *CIL* 10.1634 (116), a dedication by the *cultores Iovis Heliopolitani Berytenses qui Puteolis consistunt.*

98 On the *stationes* on the Roman forum, see G. Gatti, *Bull. comm.* 1899, 242, and L. Cantarelli, ibid. 1900, 124–133, citing Plin., *N. H.* 16.236; Suet., *Nero* 37.1; *CIL* 6.250; and *IG* 14.1008 and 1066; on the Ostian Piazzale delle Corporazioni, Meiggs, op. cit. (above, note 60) 283–285, with refs.

99 In Rome we have the *corpus negotiantium Malacitanorum* (*CIL* 6.9677); at Tomi, the οἶκος Ἀλεξανδρέων, and at Perinthus οἱ Ἀλεξανδρεῖς οἱ πραγματευόμενοι (*IGR* 1.604; cf. L. Robert, art. cit. [above, note 73] 9; *IGR* 1.800); for οἱ πραγματευόμενοι Ῥωμαῖοι, see for example *IGR* 4.1235 and *OGIS* 532. But the whole phenomenon of ναύκληροι, πραγματευόμενοι, ἔμποροι, *negotiantes*, etc., in organized groups in foreign cities is very well known.

100 Above, chapter 1 notes 54 f.; H. Braunert, *Die Binnenwanderung . . .* (1964) 172, and other jobs sought there ἵνα ἐκεῖ ἐργασώμεθα, ibid. 175; for petty craftsmen as immigrants, like the *Neapolitani citrarii* in Rome (*CIL* 6.9258), the Alexandiran smiths and bakers in Jerusalem (*Bab. Arakin* 10b and *Yoma* 38a), or the *pelegrini pictores* at Savaria (*CIL* 3.4222), see below, p. 97.

101 Liban., *Or.* 11.164; 41.6.

102 MacMullen, *Aegyptus* 44 (1964) 190; Meiggs, *Ostia* 147 f., 252, 255 f. The shrinking of town populations in the western provinces in the third and later centuries is of course well documented.

103 In Puteoli, note the *vici Vestoriani et Calpurniani* or the

regio Hortensiana, after great property-owners there, C. Dubois, *Pouzzoles antique* (1907) 46 and 51 f., and Frederiksen, art. cit. (above, note 92) 2057; for Cicero as a property-owner in Puteoli, see J. H. D'Arms, *AJP* 88 (1967) 199; in Rome, *Ad Att.* 12.32.2; 16.1.5; *Ad Q. frat.* 2.4.3; for Trimalchio's properties, Petr., *Sat.* 71.

104   On a census taken *per dominos insularum,* see Suet., *Iul.* 41.3; on bequeathing *ostiarii, topiarii, diaetarii,* and *aquarii domus* along with the building, see *Dig.* 33.7.12.42; for Cicero's remarks see *Ad Att.* 14.9.

105   *CIL* 6.67. Cf. an *officinator insulae Vitalianae* of *CIL* 6.33893 and a *popa de insula Q. Critoni* of *CIL* 6.9824; cf. 6.338 and 11.357.

106   J. Day, *Yale Class. Studies* 3 (1932) 191 f.; T. Kléberg, *Hôtels, restaurants et cabarets . . .* (1957) 50, with the review by H. T. Rowell, *AJA* 62 (1958) 124; as centers of vice and unrest, Kléberg 101 f. with refs., and MacMullen, *Enemies* 167. Whorehouses, like tenement houses, served as investments "for respectable men" (*honesti viri,* Dig. 5.3.27.1; but cf. Dio Chrysostom's view, *Or.* 14.14, that a whoremonger was hated and scorned).

107   Wilcken, Ostraka nos. 83 and 1157; Wilbour Ostraca 33; PSI 1055, lease of a municipal whorehouse by two whoremongers; other texts gathered in G. Lopuszanski, *AC* 20 (1951) 10 f., and A. Chastagnol, *Bonner Historia-Augusta-Colloquium 1964/65* (1966) 48–52, including OGIS 674, *CIL* 3.13750, Suet., *Calig.* 40 f., etc.

108   In Pompeii the *cellae meretriciae* are listed in H. Eschebach, *Die städtebauliche Entwicklung Pompeji* (1970) 175, the brothels listed in pages 174 f.

109   Matth. 26.11; Firm. Matern., *Math.* 4.14.3 (with similar texts gathered in MacMullen, *Ancient Soc.* 2 [1971] 115 f.); Greg. Nyss., *De pauper. amand.* 1 (*PG* 46.457); cf. Aug., *Sermo* 345.1, the rich scorn "the poor man lying by the door."

110   Sen., *Ad Helv.* 12.1; cf. scenes of beggary in Rome and Italy, App., *B. C.* 2.120; Juv., *Sat.* 5.8; and in Rhodes, "the masses of the poor," τὸ τῶν πενήτων πλῆθος, Strabo 14.2.5.

111   Della Corte, op. cit. (above, note 19) 151, on a location near the south corner of the forum.

CHAPTER IV

1   A well-known difficulty meets us here: does the term *eques Romanus* in inscriptions mean *equo publico* or simply anyone possessing the minimum wealth? I assume the former— see R. Duncan-Jones, *PBSR* 35 (1967) 149 f., and T. P. Wiseman, *Historia* 19 (1970) 67 ff.—while adopting in my text the looser meaning of literary usage. S. J. DeLaet's total for the *equites*, which he offers very tentatively in *Rev. belge de philol.* 20 (1941) 511 n.1, was evidently meant to include the rank as defined by pure wealth, but including the western provinces that our study excludes. It still falls below the estimate of J. Gagé, *Les classes sociales dans l'empire romain* (1964) 41, who supposes a total of a few tens of thousands. Our data may be too scant to be used. Strabo 3.5.3 says that both Cadiz and Padua had over 500 *equites* each, the former city containing, all told, over 50,000 inhabitants (P. Lavedan and J. Hugueney, *Histoire de l'urbanisme: antiquité*² [1966] 356), the latter equally large. Strabo 3.5.7 calls it the second city of Italy—larger, then, than Aquileia, which grew as Padua declined and certainly came to exceed 100,000, larger than Capua, which spread over thrice the area of Pompeii (Lavedan and Hugueney 351). By way of comparison, we may recall that *equites* approach 2 percent among the names in inscriptions of Scupi (A. Mocsy, *Gesellschaft und Romanisation in der römischen Provinz Moesia Superior* [1970] 71–73 and 162), while in Cyrene in 7 B.C. only 215 Roman citizens had as much as 2,500 denarii (*FIRA*² 1.404). As to the subsistence level, I set an approximate minimum at 250 denarii per year to support a laborer and small family in poverty, on the basis of J. Szilagyi, *Acta antiqua* 11 (1963) 347 f.; *ESAR* 1.384 f.; 4.180–183; D. Sperber, *Journ. Econ. and Soc. Hist. of the Orient* 8 (1965) 250 f.; 9 (1966) 190 f.; and R. Duncan-Jones, *PBSR* 33 (1965) 221–223. But the data need discussion for which there is no space here.

2   This is not the place to try to modify in any detail the views of scholars that I disagree with. I may just mention what seems to me an overemphasis on the profits of the middleman, adopted by M. Rostovtzeff (see above, chapter 2 note 66, and below, notes 24 f.), and an overemphasis on the scale of manufacturing, adopted by T. Frank (*ESAR* 1.291; 5.196, 198, 202 f., and 212, arguing, without or against evidence, for the existence of "factories"). Two statistics seem to me very illuminating: the more than 300 women's slippermakers in Rome (*CIL* 6.9404, already referred to), and the more than 300 traders in iron operating over a span of perhaps a decade in a small town of Noricum. Typically, they dealt in quantities that called for a capital investment only in a string of a dozen mules. See R. Egger, *Die Stadt auf dem Magdalensberg* (1961) 6–19, 22–27, and 31–34.

3   For wealth being defined mostly in rural properties, see above, chapter 1 notes 64, 73, and 88, and chapter 2 note 64; for the needed *census* of a decurion, Plin., *Ep.* 1.19, which A. N. Sherwin-White, in his note *ad loc.,* calls "the only evidence for the amount of the property qualification for municipal councillors in Italy." R. Duncan-Jones, *PBSR* 33 (1965) 201, adduces other texts not relevant but agrees that the amount may not have been uniform throughout the peninsula. Sherwin-White continues, "This passage may also indicate that Pliny assumed that most local councillors were not worth much more than the minimum franchise, which was the value of only a moderate farm." For the size of *curiae,* see *FIRA*² 1.189 lines 19 f. and Duncan-Jones 211 for the west (including an example of a 30-member *curia*) and N. Jacobone, *Un antica grande città dell'Apulia: Canusium* (1925) 173–177, showing 152 decurions in A.D. 223— more accurately interpreted as the normal 100 (with patrons and aspirants counted in) by M. G. Jarrett, *AJP* 92 (1971) 515; ibid. 514, for *curiae* of a like size in Africa. For *curiae* = *boulai,* see *ESAR* 4.814.

4   *ILS* 6090 = *FIRA*² 1.455; cf. the preceding note; *Dig.* 50.2.12 (Callistratus) referring generally to "the lack of

those who must assume civic office by necessity"; and *FIRA*[2] 1.147 lines 87 f. The lack of decurions after A.D. 250 is of course notorious.

5 Mocsy 165 finds in the inscriptions of a half-dozen chief Moesian cities that decurions represent around 8 percent, being therefore some far smaller portion of a total citizenry in which many lacked the means to buy their tombstone. Similar studies along the same lines as this would be welcome for other areas. For the total wealth of cities, Lucian, *Peregrinus* 14, is suggestive.

6 *IGR* 3.804 (cf. *ESAR* 4.780, one man's total gifts to various cities exceed 600,000 denarii; for Pliny's total in charity, Duncan-Jones 193); *ESAR* 5.58, for Seneca's fortune (cf. ibid. 24 and 27 for other fortunes of 50–75,000,000 denarii). Cicero (*Paradox. Stoic.* 49) counts an income of 150,000 denarii as luxurious, derived (if at 5 percent) from an estate of 12,000,000.

7 P. A. Brunt, *Italian Manpower* (1971) 124, guessing at a rather high figure for slaves in Italy under Augustus and at a decidedly low figure for the peninsula's total, suggests a ratio of 3 out of 7.5 millions. Other scholars do not set the slave percentage quite so high—note P. Salmon's remarks in his review of Brunt, *Latomus* 31 (1972) 920—and agree that in any case it diminished over those centuries of the Empire with which we are chiefly concerned. I do not pretend to control the subject, recently covered by J. Vogt, *Bibliographie zur antiken Sklaverei* (1971), but I have happened on a few probes into the evidence: for Africa, suggesting that 8 percent may be a representative figure for slaves in the population, see J. Marion, *Bull. d'arch. marocaine* 4 (1960) 182; cf. one slave and one freedman in the 1,271 names of a town cemetery, Castellum Celtianum, studied by H.-G. Pflaum, in *Carnuntina*, ed. E. Swoboda (1956) 126–151; and for Egypt, suggesting the figure of 10 percent, see M. Hombert and C. Préaux, *Recherches sur le recensement dans l'Egypte romaine* (1952) 170.

8 S. Gsell, *Mélanges Gustave Glotz* (1932) 398 n.6; W. L.

Westermann, *The Slave Systems of Greek and Roman Antiquity* (1955) 86; and R. MacMullen, *Ancient Society* 2 (1971) 116.

9 R. Etienne and G. Fabre, *Recherches sur les structures sociales dans l'antiquité classique, Caen 1969* (1970) 90–93, show the better life-expectancy of imperial slaves, whose children were also more likely to survive birth (T. Frank, *AHR* 21 [1916] 697).

10 For penury in horoscopes, see MacMullen, art. cit. 110 n.38 and 115; as to analogies, D. Herlihy, *Medievalia et humanistica²* 1 (1970) 98, finds 31 percent of the population of Florence propertyless in 1427, and M. Mollat, in an unpublished paper read to a symposium on poverty in the Middle Ages (Center for Medieval Studies, University of Toronto, Oct. 30, 1971), suggested on the basis of extensive studies that 20–50 percent of the urban population of western Europe at the end of the Middle Ages should be defined as poor, in the sense given in my text. I owe this last reference to the kindness of my colleague, Jeremy Adams.

11 The really hideous mortality rates discovered in dozens of studies of inscriptions are well known. For bibliography, see Etienne and Fabre, art. cit. (above, note 9) 81–97, and A. E. Samuel et al., *Death and Taxes* (1971) 6–10 and 14 f., adding S. Applebaum, *Scripta Hierosolymita* (Hebrew Univ.) 7 (1961) 44 f., showing 50 percent mortality before age 20.

12 On *obaerarii,* see above, chapter 2 note 25. Note as testimony the frequent burning of records of indebtedness when opportunity offered, for example, in time of riots (Jos., *Bell. Jud.* 7.61; Cic., *Pro Archia* 4.8; *SIG³* 684; and G. Downey, *A History of Antioch* [1961] 205 n.20).

13 *ESAR* 1.324 f.

14 B. Dobson, *Ancient Society* 3 (1972) 198, the figures being largely conjectural but the arguments (with full bibliography) quite convincing.

15 See the plans and text of G. Webster, *The Roman Imperial Army* (1969) 191 f. and 194 f.

16 P. Yale Inv. 296 (217), representing the entirety of the village's holdings according to J. F. Oates, *Proc. XII Int. Congr.*

of Papyrology (1970) 385—with my thanks to Professor Oates for permission to refer to his unpublished transcript of the papyrus; P. Lon. 604B (47); P. Cairo Isidore 6 (300/305); and F. G. DePachtère, *Mél. Rome* 28 (1908) 374 f. If we extend our probe into the later Empire, conditions appear the same. In P. Flor. 71 (second quarter of the fourth century), 22 of 33 Hermopolites own 30–100 *arourai,* 6 own 100–199, and 7 own 200–600.

17 Duncan-Jones, art. cit. (above, note 3) 280–284.

18 Cic., *Pro Sestio* 30 and *In Pis.* 17; for the habit of mind that sets βουλή and δῆμος apart, nothing is more striking than the two shown shaking hands on the coinage of Tios, in P. R. Franke, *Kleinasien zur Römerzeit* (1968) 47 no. 131, evidently in reconciliation after estrangement; but there are texts a-plenty to match this, especially epigraphic: besides Epict. 3.24.99 and Dio Chrysos., *Or.* 34.20 and 50.3, the separate honoring of the two in *TAM* 2.175 f., and the recurrent formula, "it seems good to the senate and people." Legal texts likewise oppose *curia* and *populus* or *decurio* and *plebs: Dig.* 22.5.3 pr.; 48.19.10; 48.19.2 and 5. For a wider statement, note the view that there exist in the world only "the great" and "the little," "the people" and "the wealthy" (A. Büchler, *Political and Social Leaders of . . . Sephoris* [1909] 11 n.4), of the second century; Petron., *Sat.* 44, *maiores maxillae* eat well in famine-time, not so the *populus minutus;* Lucian, *The Cock* 22, contrasting "the rich" with a typical member of the *demos,* whose earnings incidentally suggest an annual income of about 250 denarii, the subsistence level; and Philostr., *Vita Apoll.* 8.7.11, where classes are equated with ἔθνη. On the role of a city's tiny elite in equipping it with a full complement of public buildings, see Appendix C.

19 On the rural-urban exchange, see above, chapter 2 notes 59 f.; on artisans, above, chapter 3 note 100 and such rather rare examples as G. Tchalenko, *Villages antiques de la Syrie du Nord* 1 (1953) 51 and 51 n.2; 127 n.4; *CIL* 5.785; 13.5154; *AE* 1947, no. 184; *CIG* 2025 (a mosaicist who "exercised his trade in every city"); J. Ward Perkins, *JRS* 31 (1941) 104

(Greek masons in Rome) and 38 (1948) 74 (Greek sculptors in Lepcis Magna); *ILS* 7603; and W. M. Ramsay, *The Social Basis of Roman Power in Asia Minor* (1940) 95. Philostr., *Vit. soph.* 553, speaks of a major flow of young men from the north seeking jobs in Athens in his day.

20 Firm. Matern., *Math.* 5.3.50, is typical; see MacMullen, *Ancient Society* 2 (1971) 109 and 115.

21 C. G. Montefiore and H. Loewe, *A Rabbinic Anthology* (1938) 444; cf. S. Krauss, *Talmudische Archäologie* 2 (1911) 254, finding it normal for fathers to teach their sons their own craft, producing family businesses down the generations. Joseph and Jesus, both carpenters, illustrate the custom (Matt. 13.55 and Mk. 6.3). The absence of alternatives to ones' trade by inheritance underlies Libanius' assumption (*Or.* 41.6) that one threw up the craft of one's parents only to live in idleness.

22 PSI 53 cols. VII and XI, etc.; more generally, S. Calderini, *Aegyptus* 26 (1946) 19, showing that apprentice contracts to weaving often involved the sons of weavers, not a change of profession from the family's, though it is also common for sons to depart into other trades (idem, *La composizione della famiglia . . .* [1923] 30); and M. V. Biscottini, *Aegyptus* 46 (1966) 62 f., esp. 64 f., on weaving as hereditary in small shops as opposed to the freer hiring at larger ones.

23 Husband-and-wife teams appear in Rome and Cos—S. Panciera, *Archeologia classica* 22 (1970) 131, and *IGR* 4.1071; for *fratres pigmentarii* in the capital, see *CIL* 6.9796; for *sigillata* of family firms, *CIL* 11.6700, 764 (Vibieni) and 11.8119, 50 (Sceunii); for Monte Testaccio's evidence, *CIL* 15.3984, 3999, 4045, and J. Crook, *Law and Life of Rome* (1967) 229; for the βαφεῖς of Thyatira honoring a magistrate ἐπιστησάμενον τοῦ ἔργου ἀπὸ γένους τὸ ἔκτον, see *IGR* 4.1265. For heritability of agricultural labor, see for example P. Flor. 80 and PSI 789 (family groups of harvesters) and above, chapter 1 note 67.

24 Above, note 2; M. H. Callender, *Roman Amphorae* (1965) 50, on atomization of Spanish wine commerce; and D. E. L. Haynes and P. E. D. Hirst, *Porta Argentariorum* (1939) 8, on great numbers of petty brokers in Rome.

25 Callender 94, 167, and 183; P. Veyne, *Mél. Rome* 70 (1958)
    212; *RE* s.v. Handel und Industrie (H. Gummerus 1916)
    1487 f.; and H. Bloch, *I bolli laterizi* (1947) passim.
26 For bakeries, see *ESAR* 5.255; for fulleries, ibid. 262; T. P.
    Wiseman, *New Men in the Roman Senate* (1971) 91; W. O.
    Moeller, *Historia* 19 (1970) 85 n.5; Mart. 3.59. For other oc-
    cupations yielding sizable wealth, note Aul. Gell. 15.4.3
    (*mulio*), *ESAR* 5.255 (a fish-packer and a dyer), *CIL*
    14.2408 (an actor) and 2793 (a silk-dealer), *CIL* 6.9433 (a
    jeweler) and 1925 (a goldsmith), Lucian, *Somnium* 9 and
    Juv., *Sat.* 1.24 and 10.224 (barbers).
27 *ESAR* 5.254; C. Dubois, *Pouzzoles antique* (1907) 46, 49,
    and 51 f.; *RE* s.v. Puteoli (M. W. Frederiksen 1959) 2049;
    Juv., *Sat.* 1.102–106; Firm. Matern., *Math.* 5.4.20; Y. K. Ko-
    losovskaya, *Vestnik drevnei istorii* 2 (1971) 58 f.
28 *Dig.* 50.2.12 (Callistratus).
29 Petr., *Sat.* 46.
30 SHA *Firmus* 3.2 f.
31 *Pro Rabirio* 40.
32 Lucian, *Navig.* 13, 16, and 18 f.; for a representative picture
    of how Romans viewed the risks of sea trade, see Juv., *Sat.*
    14.292–302.
33 Philostr., *Vita Apoll.* 4.32.
34 *CIL* 6.9659.
35 A rereading of *SEHRE*[2] and of lesser economic histories
    will show, I think, how the accident of source-survival has
    pushed Italy forward as equivalent to "Roman Civilization."
    But even in Italy, while we await proper studies of upper-
    class continuity in places like Pompeii, Puteoli, Aquileia, and
    Milan, we can sense something close to stagnation. See G. A.
    Mansuelli, *Atti del settimo congr. int. di arch. class. 1958*
    (1961) 2.340, on Ariminum and Sarsina in the first two
    centuries A.D.; R. Meiggs, *Roman Ostia* (1960) 191 f., on the
    first-century city, and, on tell-tale iteration in the *patronatus*
    of *collegia*, J.-P. Waltzing, *Etude historique sur les corpora-
    tions professionnelles chez les Romains* 1 (1895) 398, 408,
    and 444.
36 LeBas-Wadd. 656 and 1609a. For stability in the upper class
    of second-century Athens and fourth-century Antioch, see M.

Woloch, *Historia* 18 (1969) 503, and P. Petit, *Libanius et la vie municipale à Antioche* (1955) 33 and 330; for the significance of the phrase ἀπὸ προγόνων, see D. Magie, *Roman Rule in Asia Minor* (1950) 1504 f., and A. H. M. Jones, *The Greek City* (1940) 180 f., with some interesting further observations on eastern cities in note 49, p. 342 (the equivalent phrase in Latin, as in *CIL* 9.1591, would honor a Beneventan *patronus . . . ab atavis;* cf. *CIL* 14.3614, a patron of Tibur for the third generation). Stability of the curial class is shown at Gigthis and Volubilis and sensed in other African cities by Jarrett, op. cit. (above, note 3) 532–536.

37 Lucian, *Timon* 20 f., paraphrased.

38 For sudden wealth from marriage or inheritance, see Vettius Valens (ed. W. Kroll) pp. 41 f.; Ptol., *Tetrabiblos* 4.2.174; Firm. Matern., *Math.* 3.5.19; 3.6.9; 3.7.17; 3.10.2 and 10; 3.12.3, 7, 14 and 18; 4.9.2 and 5; 4.10.4; etc. For legacy-hunting as the Roman national pastime, see the nearly one hundred refs. from dozens of Greek and Latin authors of the first century B.C. to the fourth A.D. gathered in L. Friedländer, *Roman Life and Manners*[6] (1913) 4.404 f. I can add only Cic., *De off.* 3.18.74, and a random sampling of specific fortunes assembled by the chance of mortality: Cic., *Pro Flacco* 85; *Pro Rabirio* 38 f.; Plin., *Ep.* 2.20; SHA *Maximus and Balbinus* 7.4. On key marriages, see Philostr., *Vit. soph.* 548 and Apul., *Apol. passim.* Landholding records offer another kind of evidence, for the role of marriages in the creation of a great estate, best seen in F. G. DePachtère, *La table hypothécaire de Veleia* (1920) passim, esp. 81 f. and 96.

39 Petr., *Sat.* 116.

40 Above, chapter 2 note 67.

41 I quote from B. Rawson, *CP* 61 (1966) 82; cf. L. R. Taylor, *AJP* 82 (1961) 118 f., on the poor in Rome. For the rich in Pompeii, see J. Day, *Yale Class. Studies* 3 (1932) 178. In the two areas of Italy whose landholdings are summarized in fig. 2 in text, one-eighth of the lots belonged to freedmen or persons of freedman descent: P. Garnsey, *Historia* 17 (1968) 368 f.

42 The prominence of freedmen in provincial aristocracies is

well known. I instance two areas where study reveals some sense of ratio: J. Wilkes, *Dalmatia* (1969) 234, confirmed from the northeastern provinces in a less precise way by Kolovskaya, art. cit. (above, note 27) 57–70, describing Pannonia, with *RE* Suppl. 9 s.v. Pannonia (A. Mocsy 1962) 715, and for the lower Danube, Mocsy, op. cit. (above, note 1) 90, 156, and 165 f. For a town in Africa, see G. Charles Picard, *Karthago* 8 (1957) 90.

43 Tac., *Ann.* 13.26; on a freedman uniform suggested, ibid. 13.27; for the abolitionist's wish, W. L. Rose, *Rehearsal for Reconstruction* (1964) 369, and 129 f. on the need for servility in a slave. The quotation recalls Tacitus' calling clients and freedmen *pars populi integra et magnis domibus adnexa* (*Hist.* 1.4, in contrast to his usual view of the *plebs sordida, vulgus imperitum* and *inops, Hist.* 1.4; 3.31; *Ann.* 2.77). Compare also Cicero's condescending approval of clients, *Pro Murena* 69. For *operae* due to former masters, A. M. Duff, *Freedmen in the Early Roman Empire* (1928) 44–46 and 91–94. For shock implicit in the most extreme possible violation of the code, see the revenge taken on behalf of a man "murdered by his own freedman," J. and L. Robert, *REG* 65 (1952) 179. (Hor., *Ep.* 1.1.99 f., is more lighthearted.)

44 M. Reinhold, *Historia* 20 (1971) 288; P. R. C. Weaver, *CQ* 58 (1964) 312 f.; cf. T. Frank, *AHR* 21 (1916) 692: "Apparently some names had acquired such sordid associations that they were in general avoided by ordinary [not noble, but freeborn] plebeians."

45 *IGR* 3.800 and 802: freedmen named below citizens; excluded entirely, *IG* 12, 5.663 and 667 (freedwomen) and *CIL* 10.3759; by gracious exception counted together with freeborn citizens, *IG* 12, 3.104 and *CIL* 10.5853. In Palestine, note the separation of status in *Bab. Kiddushin* 69a and Acta apost. 6.9. In Suet., *Gramm.* 18, note the formality implied in the phrase *ordo libertinus;* and in *CIL* 4.117, note the possibility that social prejudice compacted freedmen into some sort of conscious caste, supporting a Pompeian candidate as *princeps libertinorum.*

46   For the *libertini locus,* see Petr., *Sat.* 38; for freedmen's exclusion from legions, Suet., *Aug.* 25.2, and G. Forni, *Il reclutamento delle legioni* (1953) 115 f.; for exclusion from the decurionate and magistracies, see Reinhold 286 (*Cod. Just.* 9.21 and 31; 10.33.1) and Crook, op. cit. (above, note 23) 51. On the general contempt felt by the aristocracy toward freedmen, see Friedländer, op. cit. (above, note 38) 1.46 f. and 99; Duff 50–71; S. Dill, *Roman Society from Nero to Marcus Aurelius* (1905) 100–137; and A. Stein, *Der römische Ritterstand* (1927) 110 f.

47   On marriage forbidden and adultery punished between freed and senatorial or equestrian ranks, see *Dig.* 23.1.16 and 23.2.44 pr.; *Cod. Just.* 5.4.28; Suet., *Iulius* 48 and *Aug.* 67.2. Decurions were forbidden to marry slave women, *Cod. Just.* 5.5.3 (319). P. R. C. Weaver, *Past and Present* 37 (1967) 8, found that in Rome less than 15 percent of freedmen who married did so with freeborn women. Yet freedmen in Egypt could not marry fellahin, who were beneath them (*ESAR* 2.714 section 49). On illegal freedmen-*equites,* see Reinhold 284–287 and Mart. 2.29; 5.14; and 11.37.

48   P. Veyne, *Annales. Economies, sociétés, civilisations* 16 (1961) 224; and slaves and freedmen were often found in guilds together.

49   On the sacredness of the consulship acknowledged even by non-nobles, and on ridicule or disapproval of lowly pretensions to it, the more interesting texts are Cic., *In Pis.* 18; Aul. Gell. 15.4.3; Dio 51.3.5; 72.22.1; 79.14.4; Herodian 5.1.5 and 7.1.1. On the nobility's strong sense of the fitness of things, in terms of the social hierarchy, see the valuable remarks of T. Reekmans, *Ancient Society* 2 (1971) 117–161.

50   Juv., *Sat.* 1.102–106; Cic., *Ad Q. frat.* 1.2.3; cf. Plin., *Ep.* 8.6.

51   Cic., *Pro Cnaeo Plancio* 15 (*gradus* is his term); Liban., *Or.* 48.31 (τάξις is preserved ὑπὸ τοῦ νόμου). Compare Pliny's advice, *Ep.* 9.5, "preserve the distinctions between classes and dignities" (*ordines* and *dignitates;* Cicero, *Ad Q. frat.* 1.2.3, uses *dignitas* in the same way). *Ordo* was of course the usual word, for senators *en bloc,* for equestrians, but also for *plebs* (above, note 45, and J. Béranger in *Recherches sur*

les structures sociales dans l'antiquité classique, ed. C. Nicolet [1970] 226 f.). *Ordo* by itself could also mean the senate in particular, either of Rome (ibid.) or of a municipality (aside from inscriptions, *Dig.* 50.9.3 is specially clear: *ordo = curia*). In Greek the equivalents for "class" are τάξις (LSJ s.v., and Magie, *Roman Rule* 1504), τάγμα (G. E. Bean and T. B. Mitford, *Denkschr. oesterr. Akad. der Wiss.* 102 [1970] 151; Herodian 4.2.4; LSJ s.v.; and Magie 1505), ἀξίωμα (Philo, *In Flacc.* 78), ἔθνος (Philostr., *Vita Apoll.* 8.7.11), or γένος (Magie 1505).

52 *Consulares autem feminas dicimus consularium uxores (Dig.* 1.9.1.1); *clarissima puella* and *femina (CIL* 6.1848 and 3.8350); for honor inherited and marking the family down the generations, note such a phrase as γένους συγκλητικῶν, in J. Keil and A. von Premerstein, *Denkschr. oesterr. Akad. der Wiss.* 54 (1911) 26, and Dio 55.2.3, οἱ ἐκ τοῦ βουλευτικοῦ γένους ὄντες. Συγκλητικός is the more usual word in inscriptions for Roman senatorial status (*OGIS* 499; *IGR* 3.474; LeBas-Wadd. 1597 and 1708; etc.). At the municipal level we have LeBas-Wadd. 1609a (ἀρχικῶν); *IGR* 3.833b (τάγμα βουλευτικόν); *quinquennalicii* and *aedilicii (CIL* 9.338); *dictatorii (CIL* 14.4178c). But enough of such adjectives. *Talia dicturus vidit Cyllenius omnes / succubuisse oculos adopertaque lumina somno* (Ov., *Met.* 1.713 f.).

53 On titles, see H.-G. Pflaum in *Recherches* (cit. above, note 51) 164 f. and 177–182; idem, *Les procurateurs équestres sous le Haut-Empire* (1950) 167; Stein, op. cit. (above, note 46) 97–99, 101–105, and 420 f.; R. Cagnat, *Cours d'épigraphie latine*[3] (1898) 89, 109, 117, and 477; and C. Nicolet, *L'ordre équestre* 1 (1966) 256 f. Most titles became frozen really hard and fast in the second century.

54 Senatorial women were the subject of legislation concerning many details of appearance: Suet., *Iulius* 43.1 and *Domit.* 8.3; SHA *Elagabalus* 4.4; and Dio 57.15.4.

55 In addition to the *latus clavus* as opposed to the equestrian *angustus clavus,* and the toga itself that *peregrini* were forbidden (Reinhold, art. cit. [above, note 44] 282), senators wore a *luna* on their shoes (Philostr., *Vit. soph.* 555; Juv.,

Sat. 7.192; Plut., *Moral.* 470C, where I take πατρικίους to mean only "senatorial"; for discussion and recent bibliography, see G. Dossin, *Hommages à Marcel Renard* [1969] 2.240 f.) and on occasion other uniforms—the *toga praetexta,* or all-purple, etc. (Reinhold 283; *FIRA²* 1.181). I suppose regions differed also in dress and appearance. Beyond the obvious Gallic trousers and Greek chiton, Greek slaves wore a pigtail reserved in Egypt for youths of the aristocracy (Lucian, *Navig.* 2 f.), and Statius (*Silvae* 4.45 f.) hints at African differences in costume. Funerary reliefs offer a quantity of evidence never explored comparatively.

56 Many references to proud retinues: e.g. Juv., *Sat.* 1.46 and 7.142; Amm. Marc. 14.6.9; 28.2.13; and 28.4.8 f.; Firm. Matern., *Math.* 5.1.24.

57 Sen., *Contr.* 5.2.1.

58 On class differences in speech, see Petr., *Sat.* 46, *pauperorum verba derides;* Quint. 1.5.56 (on the word *gurdos*); L. R. Palmer, *The Latin Language* (1954) 151 f.; MacMullen, *Journ. Theol. Studies* 17 (1966) 110 f.; and on regional differences, above, chapter 2 notes 5–9, and Strabo 8.1.2.

59 On οἱ ἀπὸ γυμνασίου in Egypt, see S. L. Wallace, *Taxation in Roman Egypt* (1938) 403–405, and P. Jouguet, *La vie municipale dans l'Egypte romaine* (1911) 79–86.

60 G. W. Bowersock, *Greek Sophists in the Roman Empire* (1969) 22–24, and F. Millar, *JRS* 59 (1969) 16 f. and 19 f.

61 Γένει καὶ πλούτῳ is the phrase in Euseb., *H. E.* 7.15.1 (cf. 7.16.1) and Greg. Nyss., *Vita S. Greg. Thaum.* (*PG* 46.921), with a similar pairing in laudatory decrees: A. Wilhelm, *JOAI* 28 (1933) 57 f.; *SIG³* 800; and above, note 36. I have looked in vain for a match to such phrases in Latin inscriptions or texts prior to A.D. 300.

62 M. G. Jarrett, *Historia* 12 (1963) 210 f., on names in *-ianus* from Africa, and, more generally, J. Marion, *Bull. d'arch. marocaine* 4 (1960) 136–138. On the development of such formations among imperial slaves in the first to second centuries, see Weaver, art. cit. (above, note 44) 315. On craftsman names like "Faber," see G. Kuehn, *De opificum Romanorum condicione privata* (1910) 24 f.; C. Humann et al.,

Altertümer von Hierapolis (1898) 155; H. Gummerus, *Jb. deut. arch. Inst.* 28 (1913) 90 n.5 and 91; and above, chapter 1 note 56.

63 *Nomen = gens,* in *ILS* 8274–7278; *CIL* 6.10701, 19844, 28318; *Dig.* 50.16.195.2; Cic., *Topica* 6.29; on *falsi nominis vel cognominis adseveratio,* see *Dig.* 48.10.13 pr. (Papinian); on change of name to fit a change in status, see Lucian, *The Cock* 14 and *Timon* 22.

64 Ἔχων ἐστὶ in N. Lewis, *TAPA* 90 (1959) 140; for the status of veterans, ranked as decurions, *Dig.* 49.18.3 (Marcianus) and LeBas–Wadd. 2227 and 2546, where individuals claim membership among the group οὐετρανικῶν; more generally, MacMullen, *Soldier and Civilian,* chap. 5. For illiteracy among decurions, see *Cod. Just.* 10.31.6 and Mocsy, op. cit. (above, note 1) 230.

65 Jones, *Greek City* 172 and 180 f.

66 P. Garnsey, *Social Status and Legal Privilege in the Roman Empire* (1970) 79, 208, and passim. This excellent book makes it unnecessary for me to say more on *honestiores* and *humiliores,* who would otherwise need a long discussion.

67 Less honored tribes in Ostia and Puteoli: Meiggs, *Roman Ostia* 190; cf. Cic., *Pro Sestio* 114, for Rome. For discrimination in *sportulae* there are many scores of examples, e.g. *CIL* 9.3160 and 14.2408; more generally, S. Mrozek, *Epigraphica* 30 (1968) 158–165, and A. R. Hands, *Charities and Social Aid in Greece and Rome* (1968) 91 f., both citing earlier studies. Associations in this as in other respects mirrored the larger community. See J.-P. Waltzing, *Etude historique sur les corporations professionnelles chez les Romains* 1 (1895) 305.

68 Several third-century rabbinical texts introduce the term "the Haughty." See A. Büchler, *Political and Social Leaders of . . . Sephoris* (1909) 17 f. It specially characterized Romans in the eyes of eastern provincials (Tat., *Ad Graec.* 35). Note also the gestures implied in the words ἐξυπτιάζειν and ὑπεροψία in LSJ s.vv., *superciliosus* in Latin, and descriptions of the proud "walking about stiffly upright," "strutting, disdainfully placing their hands on their hips," in M. Schwab,

Le Talmud de Jérusalem (1871) 1.405, and Euseb., *Praep. ev.* 6.41. Aug., *Enarr. in Ps.* 39.28, depicts a debt-ridden *pauper* having to apply to a *dives, cui deferre, cui venienti assurgere, quem inclinato capite salutare* [*solet*].

69 Epict. 3.14.11 f. and 14.
70 Ibid. 4.6.4, in the Loeb translation. The closest parallels may be found in Lucian, *Nigrinus* 23, and Anm. Marc. 14.6.8–10. Epictetus devotes a long passage (4.7.19–24—much more effective than any in Seneca, e.g. *Ep.* 31.11) to freeing his listeners from the scramble for rank, status, and promotion. To this contest Plutarch (*Moral.* 470C) also refers. Most people, he says, "weep because they do not wear the patrician shoe, and if they do wear it, that they are not yet Roman praetors; or if that, then because they are not consuls," etc.
71 On such scenes, of course provoked by the supine idleness of the not-very-poor, who never dreamed of taking a job, see well-known passages in Petronius' *Cena Trimalchionis,* e.g. *Sat.* 48, an example of the rich man's "outspokenness" that P. Oxy. 2554 refers to (παρρησία); further, Juv., *Sat.* 5.30 f., 146–149, and 156 f. ("Perhaps you think Virro grudges the cost" of feeding a humble guest as sumptuously as a more distinguished person; no, "He behaves this way to hurt you"); Plin., *Ep.* 2.6; and Mart. 3.82.
72 Juv., *Sat.* 3.153 f.; on laughter at cheap clothes, ibid. 147 f.; Plin., *Ep.* 9.6, *vulgus, quod vilius tunica;* and A. Büchler, *Economic Conditions of Judaea* (1912) 42 n.2, a rabbi mocked in the streets of Rome because he had no shoes. Note also *Laus Pisonis* 113 f., saying that clients in Piso's house "suffer no arrogant jests; no man's distress brings sudden laughter. . . . [But] rare is the house that does not scorn a lowly friend, nor contemptuously tread down a humble client"; Petr., *Sat.* 57; Dio Chrysos., *Or.* 7.115; Joh. Chrysos., *Hom. ad pop. Ant.* 2.8 (*PG* 49.45); Liban., *Or.* 58.4, where schoolboys jeer at a χειροτέχνης; and Greg. Nyss., *PG* 46.936 f.
73 By exception, certain prominent men affected a very democratic address to humble acquaintances in the street: Plut., *Crassus* 3.5 and *Caes.* 4.4; Petron., *Sat.* 44; Liban., *Or.* 2.6.

For the bullying drunk, cf. Juv., *Sat.* 3.296, cited in a good paragraph on the abuse of the humble by the great, in T. Reekmans, *Ancient Society* 2 (1971) 153.

74 D. Sperber, *Zeitschr. deut. morgenländischen Gesellschaft* 120 (1970) 260.

75 On the contempt of actors, see Appendix B. s.v. *mimus;* on bankrupts publicly disgraced, see Cic., *Phil.* 2.18.44; *FIRA*² 1.149; Vett. Valens 42; and J. M. Kelly, *Roman Litigation* (1966) 21–23. On τελῶναι, MacMullen, *Ancient Society* 2 (1971) 108 and Appendix B s.v.; on *praecones,* ibid.; on public disgrace by beating (which, like the job of actor, toll-collector, or auctioneer, constituted disqualification for the decurionate of the typical Italian city) see *Dig.* 50.2.12 (Callistratus). For Caesar's sense that the poor, the dishonorable, could not be dishonored, see Sall., *Cat.* 51.12, though he is speaking here specifically of crimes of violence—*si quid iracundia deliquere.*

76 Plin., *Ep.* 9.5, discussing the *sinisteritas* of opposing the *gratia potentium.* The overtones of the letter are what count. On the actual operation of *potentes* or δυνατοί and *potentia* and δύναμις, see Ael. Arist., *Or.* 26 (*To Rome*) 65; Mac-Mullen, *Ancient Society* 2 (1971) 114; above, chapter 1 notes 31, 33, and 42 f., and 2 notes 52 and 76. On the workings of *patrocinium* (for which προξενία is no true equivalent) and of *Gratia* (for which χάρις may be used, e.g. in N. Lewis, *RIDA* 15 [1968] 137), see MacMullen, loc. cit.; E. Birley, *Roman Britain and the Roman Army* (1953) 141 f.; Pflaum, *Procurateurs* (cit. above, note 53) 197–209; and Kelly 53–60.

77 P. Mich. VIII 468 (early second century); cf. Tac., *Ann.* 1.17 and *Hist.* 1.46, and Pliny's discovery of "disgusting rapacity" in the officer ranks, *Ep.* 7.31.

78 For *Caesaris servi* with immense *peculia,* see e.g. Plin., *N. H.* 7.129; Suet., *Otho* 5.2 and *Vesp.* 23.2. For tips and bribes expected by slaves in great establishments, see Lucian, *On Salaried Posts* 14 and 37; Fronto, *Ep. ad M. Caes.* p. 68 (ed. Naber); and Hor., *Sat.* 1.9.57. Indirect evidence is overwhelming.

79 P. Fay. 117 f. (A.D. 108–110, in Egypt); *FIRA*² 1.497 (A.D.

180–183, in Africa); M. Hadas, *Philol. Quarterly* 8 (1929) 372 f., the third-century saying attributed to Roman judges in Palestine, "Bring me a δῶρον" (compare Epict. 3.7.31 and 4.6.31, you must ingratiate yourself with an influential man by sending a δῶρον); MacMullen, *HSCP* 68 (1964) 310 and 316, examples of bribe-taking in the first half of the fourth century in Egypt and Syria; and *Dig.* 1.16.6.3 (Ulpian), saying that a governor should restrict himself to receiving small presents, *ut neque morose abstineat neque avare modum xeniorum excedat.* Much evidence is gathered by Kelly, op. cit. (above, note 75) 38–41, and the significance of the word *abstinentia* in praise of civil servants is seen by Pflaum, op. cit. (above, note 53) 169—though he might more conveniently have referred to *ILS* 1176, 1192, 1390, 1433, 6244, and 6277.

80   Origen, *C. Cels.* 6.15, trans. H. Chadwick; similar passages in Lucian, *Somnium* 9 and *Nigr.* 21, and above, chapter 2 note 52. On the usual form of address to a superior, "Master" (*Domine, κύριε*), see L. Friedländer, *Roman Life and Manners*[6] (1913) 4.84 f.

81   Appendix B s.v. *vulgus.* Ὄχλος and δῆμος seem not to attract an equal scorn among Greek writers, but the Apologists correct our impression. It was a recurrent charge that Christianity was a religion for the mob, therefore contemptible. See esp. Orig., *C. Cels.* 3.18 and 75; 4.31 and 50. Both parties to that debate share the sense of distance from the masses.

82   On scorn of fullers, see DE s.v. *Fullones* 320 and Appendix B s.v. *fullo;* for weavers, ibid. s.v. ἐριουργός.

83   *Pro Flacco* 18, *opifices* and *tabernarii.*

84   Liban., *Or.* 15.77, on the rudeness to be expected of a smith or tanner; on the unsuitableness and degrading nature of *banausic* or illiberal crafts, Sen., *Ep.* 88.21 and 23, Cic., *De off.* 1.150, Dio Chrysos., *Or.* 7.110, and Lucian, *Somnium* 9.

85   See the refs. in Appendix B s.v. βαφεύς and *lanius.*

86   Cic., loc. cit.; cf. *Dig.* 7.8.4 pr.; 39.4.1.5; and 43.16.1.18— —cited by F. M. de Robertis, *Studia et documenta historiae*

et iuris 24 (1958) 270 f. and 274, to show that laborers were equated with slaves; idem, *Lavoro e lavoratori nel mondo romano* (1963) 67, citing other useful passages.

87 Val. Max. 8.14.6; Sen., *Ep.* 88.18; Plin., *N. H.* 29.17; Cic., loc. cit. (but cf. *Brutus* 73) The prejudice extended also to Greek higher culture, even religion. Cf. on rhetoric, Aul. Gell. 15.11.2; on music, Cic., *Tusc.* 1.1–2.5; on Dionysiac cult, πᾶσι πονηρὸν πλὴν δούλων, Art., *Oneir.* 2.37.

88 On *tabernarii* or merchants forced to lie for a living, see Cic., loc. cit.; Plin., *N. H.* 18.225; Julian, *Ep.* 42.442B f.; Aug., *Enarr. in Ps.* 70.17; Appendix B s.v. κάπηλος; de Robertis, *Lavoro* 55 f. On the same grounds, Dio Chrysostom holds in contempt small-time lawyers, who make their living by lying (*Or.* 7.123).

89 Dio 52.8.5; Cic., *Pro Sulla* 48; Epict. 4.1.55. That slavery even under a humane master negated pride and self-respect was its only essential evil, in the ancient mind. The times and people I write about, so far as I can discover, acknowledged no theory of the just price, therefore no such thing as "exploitation." Their lack of that moral category fitted with their acceptance of free enterprise unlimited (above, chapter 3 note 29).

90 For the argument that poverty made men venal, see texts discussed by Garnsey, op. laud. (above, note 66) 208 and 212 (esp. *Dig.* 22.5.3 and *FIRA*² 2.501), adding Tac., *Ann.* 14.14; for riches on display as being incitements to theft, see Epict. 1.18.14 and Joh. Chrysos., *In ps. XLVIII,* 2 (*PG* 55.516); for the avarice of the rich as a cause of others' poverty, see Ambrose, *De Nabuthe* 12.53 (*PL* 14.767), and Julian, *Ep.* 89b.290A; and for the recognition that the rich created crime by depriving others of a lawful subsistence, see Jos., *Ant. Jud.* 18.274; Dio 77.10.5; and Silius Italicus 13.585; for joblessness as a root of crime, Montefiore and Loewe, loc. cit. (above, note 21) and Ephesians 4.28; and for the connection between a country's inadequate natural resources and a high crime rate, Strabo 3.3.5 and 3.5.1.

91 Stoic influence, and nostalgia for Rome's early simplicity,

both produce passages in praise of poverty; but in the real world—Latin-speaking if not Greek—it was held in contempt. See Appendix B s.v. *egens.*

92 Cic., loc. cit., slightly condensed; a similar echo in Julian, *Or.* 1.15C–D; on the distinction between *mercator* and *negotiator,* ἔμπορος and κάπηλος, see Appendix B s.v. *mercator,* with refs.

93 *In Verr.* 2.3.67; 2.4.46; 2.5.15 and 154; *Cat.* 2.18; and A. W. Lintott, *Violence in Republican Rome* (1968) 37; cf. *Rep.* 1.47, the similar thought shown in the pairing, *familiarum vetustatibus aut pecuniis ponderantur,* compared with *princeps civitatis et pecunia et gratia,* Sen., *De benef.* 2.27.2— money being always the central term in the phrase.

94 Garnsey, *Social Status* 210–212 (note *Dig.* 47.2.52.21, *honestus vir = vir locuples,* and Plin., *Ep.* 1.14.9; in protest against the equation, Juv., *Sat.* 3.137 f., and Tatian, *Ad Graec.* 11); Claudius' speech on admission of Gauls to the inner sanctum of the state, *CIL* 13.1668 Col. II lines 3 f., *flos coloniarum et municipiorum, bonorum scilicet virorum et locupletiorum; attributio* to a township granted by Antoninus Pius on the basis of *vita et censu* (*CIL* 5.532; cf. *SIG*³ 880, the same reasoning *re* Pizos in 202); admission to municipal office by wealth (*Dig.* 50.4.14.3 f.) as to the Roman senate (Dio 52.19.2), by careful policy; and the assumption in Palestine that the authorities will reason, "He is rich, I shall appoint him judge" (Büchler, op. cit. [above, note 18] 30 n.1).

95 *Quaestus omnis patribus indecorus visus,* Livy 21.63.4, speaking of the Lex Claudia of 218 B.C.; but for later times, see Tac., *Hist.* 2.86: a person quits the senate before indulging his *quaestus cupido.*

96 Compare the reservations expressed about wealth with the means chosen to gain it for oneself, in Sall., *Cat.* 12.1 (cf. Dio 43.9.2), Cic., *Paradox. Stoic.* 49 or *Rep.* 1.51 (cf. J. Carcopino, *Les secrets de la correspondance de Cicéron* [1947] Part I chapters 1–2), and Sen., *Epp.* 17, 87, and 115 passim (cf. Dio 62.1). Similar strictures on the greed for money are expressed in the second century in Ps.-Sall., *Ep. ad Caes.*

2.7.3–10 (for the date, see R. Syme, *Mus. Helveticum* 15 [1958] 54), and Lucian, *Nigrinus* 23, and again in the fourth century, in Julian, *Ep.* 89.453C, and Joh. Chrysos., *Hom.* 34.5 f. (*PG* 61.292–296). I omit as being strangely encapsulated in the Roman mind the view that the Republic declined as *luxus* grew. That was ancient history for Cicero and later writers (for the texts, see Polyb. 18.34.7 f.; Sall. *Bell. Jug.* 1, 15 f., and 41 f.; Val. Max. 4.4.11; Plin., *N. H.* 33.53; Juv., *Sat.* 6.287–300; Plut., *Moral.* 88A; and Tac., *Ann.* 3.54).

97 E. Magaldi, *Atti Accad. Pontaniana* 60 (1930) 62, with the inscription elsewhere, *lucrum gaudium*.

98 Juv., *Sat.* 14.201–204; cf. Suet., *Vesp.* 23.3, and, less close a parallel, Hor., *Ep.* 1.1.53 f., *quaerenda pecunia primum est: virtus post nummos.*

99 Pecunia worshiped, Hor., *Ep.* 1.6.37; Juv. 1.113; SHA *Quad. tyr.* 8.6, on the Alexandrians: *unus illis deus nummus est;* and Aug., *Civ. dei* 4.21 and 24; 7.3 and 11 f. These passages in Latin thought are not matched in Greek, where Philotimia ("the worst of the gods," Eur., *Phoenissae* 532) bears a double meaning, one part of which embodies a tradition of largesse (above, chapter 3 note 14).

100 A. R. Hands, *Charities and Social Aid in Greece and Rome* (1968) chapter 7 passim; Waltzing, op. laud. (above, note 35) 1.302; above, note 67. *IGR* 3.800 offers a good illustration of "charity" according to status, including as it does a fund for the rearing of orphans.

101 Despair of curing poverty is heard from Dio Chrysostom (*Or.* 7.125, slightly changed in my translation) and Seneca (*De vita beata* 24); for *iners* and ἀργός, see Hands 65 and MacMullen, *Ancient Society* 2 (1971) 110 n.38; for the graffito, see *CIL* 4.9839b.

102 Sall., *Cat.* 37.3; Cic., *De off.* 2.24.85; Lucian, *The Cock* 22; *Saturnalia* 31; *Navigium* 27; Plut., *Moral.* 822A; Herodian 7.3.5; Art., *Oneir.* 4.17; Aug., *Serm.* 345.1.

103 In perhaps the best-known of many modern books on Roman society, J. Carcopino, *Daily Life in Ancient Rome* (1941) 66, here swallows Juv., *Sat.* 9.140 entire.

104 A. Bernardi, in *The Economic Decline of Empires,* ed. C. M. Cipolla (1970) 34 and n.6; F. Walbank, *The Awful Revolution* (1969) 45, "The Romans despised the free artisan as doing work proper to a slave"; C. Mossé, *The Ancient World at Work* (1969) 28, referring to "the scorn felt for the artisan . . . , the contempt accorded to manual or mercantile occupations." De Robertis, *Lavoro* 47, rightly called this the *communis opinio* and rightly avoided it.

105 Petron., *Sat.* 29. Compare likewise the contempt for various occupations expressed in the references in Appendix B, with the unashamed specification of these same occupations in inscriptions and tomb-reliefs: a *mango* (*IGR* 4.1257), a *lanarius* (*CIL* 11.741), a *tonsor* (*CIL* 6.9940), a *nummularius* (*CIL* 6.9709), a *praeco* (*CIL* 1.1210), etc. H. Gummerus, *Jb. deut. arch. Inst.* 28 (1913) 68–91, gives a fine selection of reliefs. Cf. de Robertis, *Lavoro* 31 and 34–36, A. T. Geoghegan, *The Attitude towards Labor . . .* (1945) 51–53, and J. P. V. D. Balsdon, *Life and Leisure in Ancient Rome* (1969) 135, who all draw the obvious conclusions—against the *communis opinio* of the preceding note. Rabbis especially defended labor. The third-century quotation in the text is representative (from C. G. Montefiore and H. Loewe, *A Rabbinic Anthology* [1938] 444; cf. also *Bab. Megillah* 12b; *Yebamoth* 118b; *Kiddushin* 82b; *Nedarim* 49b; *Aboth* 1.10; *Berak* 8a; and W. Baron, *A Social and Religious History of the Jews*[2] [1952] 2.256, and Geoghegan 75).

CHAPTER V

1 *On Salaried Posts* 25.

2 For the well-defined sense of place, see above, chapter 4 notes 43 and 51, and *Dig.* 38.1.34 (Pomponius) on remission of *operae* due from a freedwoman, "if she rises to such a *dignitas* that it is unsuitable for her to render them."

3 Differences in manners and values between the Latin- and the Greek-speaking parts of our area of study appear above, chapter 3 note 69, and 4 notes 61, 68, 91, and 99. The prevalence of caricatures of nations and city-state populations

can best be illustrated by passages dealing with Alexandrians and (usually meaning the same thing) Egyptians: Tac., *Hist.* 1.11; Plin., *Paneg.* 31.2; Dio Chrysos., *Or.* 32.1, 68, 77 and 86; Herodian 4.9.2; Dio 51.17.1; *Expositio tot. mundi* 37; etc.; and more generally E. Wölfflin in *Archiv für Lat. Lexicographie* 7 (1892) 135–146, 333–342.

4 Dio Chrysos., *Or.* 7.100, 102, 107, 110 f., and 128 f.; Amm. Marc. 28.1.15; and M. Bloch, *Annales d'hist. écon. et sociale* 6 (1934) 307.

SELECT BIBLIOGRAPHY

From several hundred modern works cited in the notes, I list here only a very few of special value for the present essay, through their methods or scope.

H. Braunert, *Die Binnenwanderung. Studien zur Sozialgeschichte Ägyptens in der Ptolemäer- und Kaiserzeit,* 1964.

M. Della Corte, *Case ed abitanti di Pompei*[2], 1954.

ESAR. See Abbreviations.

L. Friedländer, *Roman Life and Manners under the Early Empire,* trans. L. A. Magnus, ed. 7, 1908–09.

P. Garnsey, *Social Status and Legal Privilege in the Roman Empire,* 1970.

Recherches sur les structures sociales dans l'antiquité classique, Caen 1969, 1970.

F. M. de Robertis, *Lavoro e lavoratori nel mondo romano,* 1963.

SEHRE[2]. *See* Abbreviations.

P. Veyne, "Vie de Trimalcion," *Annales. Economies, sociétés, civilisations* 16 (1961) 213–247.

J.-P. Waltzing, *Etude historique sur les corporations professionelles chez les Romains,* 1895–1900.

INDEX

The index does not list references to ancient authors in the Appendixes and Notes, nor does it include references to places that are mentioned not in the text but only in the Appendixes and Notes.

207